Love and Living Together

Love and Living Together

DALE ROBB

FORTRESS PRESS **Philadelphia**

COPYRIGHT © 1978 BY FORTRESS PRESS

All rights reserved. No part of this publication may be reproduced, stored in a retrieval system, or transmitted in any form or by any means, electronic, mechanical, photocopying, recording, or otherwise, without the prior permission of the copyright owner.

Library of Congress Cataloging in Publication Data

Robb, Dale, 1921-
   Love and living together.
   Includes bibliographical references.
   1. Marriage. 2. Love. 3. Unmarried couples.
4. Sexual ethics. I. Title.
HQ734.R595   301.42   77-15242
ISBN 0-8006-1326-0

6506L77   Printed in the United States of America   1–1326

To Arlene

Contents

An Open Letter to Jane	9
Why Marry?	11
Let's Just Live Together	21
What's Wrong with Sex?	30
What Do You Really Want?	41
What Is Love?	49
Able to Love	56
How to Reach the Altar	69
Are You Ready?	80
Can Love Survive?	89
Appendixes	99
Notes	103
Suggestions for Further Reading	107
Acknowledgments	110

An Open Letter to Jane

Dear Jane,

Last summer when you came home from college and asked to talk with me, I quickly realized how serious you were.

"Do people really need to marry?" you asked. "Isn't marriage a form of bondage? Wouldn't people be happier if they were free to enjoy love whenever they find it?"

I know you well enough to appreciate your desire for reliable answers. Among your acquaintances traditional rules of courtship and marriage are openly questioned. You know couples who have rented apartments and set up housekeeping.

You find yourself deeply puzzled. With your boyfriend, you naturally wonder if the two of you are missing an opportunity in not living together. You sense within yourself, Jane, that you are not free to cohabit without marriage. Since early childhood your parents have taught you to believe that sexual intimacy is labelled with a sign in large letters: RESERVED FOR MARRIED COUPLES!

You want to know if this rule still holds, or if it is an old-fashioned restriction which modern contraceptives have outmoded? What is the right way to enjoy/control your own exciting, enchanting capacity to love?

Your questions are urgently important. You and other thoughtful young people deserve clear, reliable answers about sex and marriage.

10   *LOVE AND LIVING TOGETHER*

In response to your need I have gathered stories of what other youth have experienced in testing different ways of relating to one another. I have changed the names and other identifying information to avoid embarrassment to those who have supplied me with information. I hope that these present-day experiences and my comments on them will help you and other young readers in finding happiness. When you have finished reading let us find a time for further conversation.

Sincerely,
Dale Robb

Why Marry?

As **George** turned to hang up the dish towel, **Ginger** ran her fingers under the dripping faucet and flipped water at him. Then, laughing heartily, she dashed from the kitchen. George accepted her challenge and pursued her.

In the living room he found her standing on the opposite side of the sofa with feet spread to allow a quick start in either direction. When George moved to the right she scampered toward the other end of the sofa. He reversed his course and she matched his move, keeping the sofa between them.

They played vigorously, Ginger skillfully keeping out of reach. Then the game ended as they knew it would—Ginger squealed and ran directly into his arms. They embraced fondly.

"George, will you marry me?"

"I did!"

"I know, but that was four weeks ago! Will you marry me tonight?"

"Of course! Will you marry me?"

"I'm glad you asked me, Dear. I never knew that it would be so wonderful!"

They seated themselves on the sofa and George said quietly, "It wasn't easy to wait for each other so long, but I'm glad we agreed to do it."

"I really don't know how we did it. You're the original love bug! On our honeymoon, you were ready to go to bed after every meal. Wow! But thanks for helping work it out our way!"

"Honey, I knew you wanted a lovely wedding. Both of us wanted a honeymoon to fulfill our love. By the way, you seemed to thrive on the honeymoon routine yourself!"

12 *LOVE AND LIVING TOGETHER*

"I guess we're both hooked on love. I'm glad we waited to be married. I can't imagine how a couple could just start living together and be happy."

Sam and **Cindy** are reclining on floor pillows in their bedroom. Six weeks earlier Cindy had come to live with Sam in a house rented cooperatively with three other unmarried people. They are listening to a new stereo cassette when Cindy speaks:

"It's fun to room with you—no quarrels, just lots of time to talk. Now we can be together every night!"

"Yeh! The fun level is way up since you came! I can't imagine why couples lock themselves into marriage when living like this is so much better!"

COHABITATION WITHOUT MARRIAGE

In America alone the number of couples living together without marriage has reached nearly a million. Two-person households made up of unrelated adults of opposite sex number 957,000, a growth of 83% in seven years.

What causes this rapid increase in cohabitation without marriage? Economic factors cause some people to "live in" without marrying. A divorcée may lose alimony by marrying. Older persons who are attracted to each other can often maintain higher income by keeping legal standing as single persons. Convenience and pleasure influence many "singles" to cohabit, but objections to marriage rank high among the reasons. The experience of Sam and Cindy is a case in point.

Sam and **Cindy** dated steadily during their senior year at the university. Sam was Jewish and Cindy came from a Baptist family. The parents on both sides were unhappy over the growing friendship and issued thinly veiled warnings that there must not be a marriage.

The parents could have spared their efforts to avoid a marriage. Sam and Cindy had no intention to marry. Sam believed in a new lifestyle in which each person could do his own thing. He did not want to tie himself to any lifelong promises which might later interfere with his own desires. Neither did he want Cindy to commit herself. He was convinced that women have long been oppressed as homemakers, wives, and mothers. The simplest way, in his opinion, to avoid injustice and to preserve personal freedom was not to marry.

Cindy had been engulfed in marital conflict as long as she could remember. Her parents intermittently argued or kept an icy silence. Two of Cindy's sisters had suffered domestic tragedy ending in divorce, bitterness, and hardship for small children and estranged adults. A third sister was very unhappy in her marriage. The marriages which Cindy knew intimately were so tragic that she resolved not to marry.

After graduation Sam found work and arranged to live in a rented house with four other single fellows. Cindy found work near her home and lived with her parents. She watched in agony as the parental conflict swirled around her, and then tried to be a daughter to both combatants after her father moved out. She and Sam talked often and at length by telephone.

One of Sam's fellow-renters took a job in another city. Sam asked the remaining threesome if they would let Cindy join the rental group as his roommate. They had no objection, so Sam telephoned to invite Cindy.

Cindy quickly sensed that she could regain happiness by accepting, but she wanted the terms to be quite clear. Over the phone she and Sam negotiated an agreement for living together:

1. They would remain financially independent in order to avoid any fighting over money or property.
2. They would cohabit but would not bear children.
3. The agreement could be ended at any time by either party.

Cindy quit work, moved her personal belongings, and set up housekeeping with Sam and his friends. She soon found a job and paid her share of the costs of room and board. Cindy and

Sam were delighted to be together. They felt that they had found an ideal balance of freedom and companionship, an arrangement in which their love would be unhindered by the entanglements of marriage.

FEAR OF MARRIAGE

Cindy was not unique in trying to avoid tragedy by refusing to marry. Marital breakdown is an alarming reality in contemporary society. In some recent years there has been one divorce for every two marriages, the divorce rate having doubled in slightly more than a decade. Often marital conflict leads to violent tragedy. One urban homicide survey disclosed that the bedroom was "the most dangerous" place in the city.

Because of the grief and disorientation which accompany marital failure, many young adults are afraid of marriage. One young social worker who was employed as a counselor for delinquent youth told his father, "Marriage is all right for you and Mom, but I work with the tragic results of bad marriages everyday and I don't want to run the risk."

In an interview Olivia Newton-John, the winner of many coveted awards as a pop singer, admitted that the possibility of marriage frightened her: "My parents, my sister, and so many of my friends have been divorced.... Also I've gotten a bit selfish. I want to see a lot and do a lot of things I haven't explored yet."

TRADITIONS UNDER ATTACK

The stormy experience of many contemporary folk in marriage is one of the major reasons for a wide-ranging attack upon standards of sex behavior and marriage. At least five distinct forces which influence attitudes can be identified:

1. Youth are testing our sex and marriage tradition. Older youth and young adults enjoy unprecedented freedom for

couples to be alone. A large percentage of youth have automobiles and job earnings or other resources to use in travel. Youth on a date are highly mobile. Chaperonage is usually not as strict as in earlier eras. Often both parents are employed, allowing youth some privacy at one home or even both homes. At the college level many institutions have established open dormitories allowing freedom for more intimate association than earlier generations knew. Owners of rental apartments in some communities rent a unit to an unmarried couple as readily as they do to a wedded couple. When this new freedom is combined with youthful eagerness to question tradition and to explore the unknown, it yields widespread experimentation in styles of living together.

Youth's quest for new lifestyles is dramatically displayed in the founding of communes. It was estimated recently that there were over three thousand communal living groups in America alone. Many communes manifest a revolt of youth against chastity and monogamy. Youth are questioning traditions and testing alternatives to established customs of sexuality.

2. Frequently, disenchanted, exmarried persons oppose the institution of marriage. Author Norman Mailer, the exhusband of five women and the father of seven children, has attributed the current sexual revolution to a "profound rejection of the American family." Mailer has maintained that a large proportion of Americans view the nuclear family founded by marriage as an "enemy" of their well-being.

3. Advocates of women's liberation often attack marriage as the root of many injustices. One coed who attended a Womens' Rights Conference returned with the staunch conviction that marriage had enslaved women. She was eagerly searching for an alternate lifestyle which would allow women to enjoy social equality and economic freedom.

4. Social scientists have called public attention to the extent of sex activity that violates the tradition of premarital chastity and have raised scholarly doubts about the custom of marriage. In the post-World War II decade Alfred Kinsey's findings about sex behavior startled many parents.

Lawrence Casler in his provocative book *Is Marriage Necessary?* has analyzed modern marriage in terms of its functions and concluded: "Whatever its origins may have been, the institution of marriage is no longer necessary for the optimal functioning of our society.... Sexual, economic, emotional, and child-rearing requirements have been shown to be readily satisfiable outside the bounds of matrimony."

Sociologist M. L. Cadwallader wrote: "The institution of marriage . . . has failed."

5. The communications media have widely advertised a great variety of alternative lifestyles. Slick paper magazines with elaborate color photographs display the human body and promote a view of human existence that features sex. A cartoonist suggested the measure of their distortion by drawing a sketch of a man and woman to the scale of a postage stamp with sex organs of lifelike dimensions.

Movies and television explore a multitude of alternate styles of living. The entertaining motion picture *I Will . . . I Will . . . for Now* featured the difficulties people encounter with premarital pregnancy, trial marriages, six-month contract marriage, and sex therapy for the married.

The TV show "Love American Style" depicted a high school couple who rented an apartment and moved in. When a pastor visited them, they explained, "We love each other now. We don't see any reason why we shouldn't enjoy our love fully. We are living and not making any promises. If we split a year from now, no one will be hurt."

We have taken sex out of the closet where it was rarely discussed in public and have flung it, like a banner, on a hilltop which everyone can see. Youth who hear, read, and see so many varied portrayals of lifestyles and so much vigorous criticism of marriage are understandably confused. Is marriage itself wrong or have people failed to learn how to be happily married? Is marriage really necessary? What are the essential functions of present day marriage?

THE CHANGING FUNCTIONS OF MARRIAGE

Investigation reveals that many of the historic functions of marriage have changed. In nineteenth century households domestic tasks required full-time homemakers. Many families raised their own vegetables and fruit. Someone, often the housewife, had to plant, cultivate, and harvest the vegetables; then she had to clean and preserve or cook them. Meat production involved raising the animal, butchering, drying, salting, or smoking the meat, and eventually frying, roasting, or broiling it. Laundry equipment usually consisted of a scrubboard, a tub, a clothesline, and clothespins. The homemaker who had several children usually spent one long day each week doing the washing. A second day was devoted to ironing or pressing the clothing.

Clothing production and upkeep was another major task—carding, spinning, weaving, and sewing were time-consuming tasks of the homemaker.

A folk song which adults taught little children reflected the strenuous routine of the week:

"Today is Monday, today is Monday.
Monday, washday!"

Succeeding verses added a new day with its particular duty as follows:

"Tuesday, iron!
Wednesday, sew!
Thursday, shop!
Friday, clean!

Saturday, bake!
Sunday, church!"

The refrain climaxed each repetition of the activity of the day with the question,

"Is everybody happy?
Well, I should say!"

A full-time homemaker was indispensable in that bygone era and often a wife hired one or more full-time or part-time helpers. A woman with daughters old enough to help was considered very fortunate. The folk wisdom of that age included a gentle jibe about the advantage of being a man:

Man works from sun to sun;
Woman's work is never done.

Families in that era were economic units engaged in farming or business enterprises where the need for workers seemed insatiable. There were woods to be cleared, crops to be tended, and stores to mind. Methods of farming and transportation were primitive, involving strenuous physical exertion. A married couple who produced many children had a distinct advantage on the frontier. Pioneer couples on the edge of a vast, sparsely populated region felt the urgent importance of childbearing.

The social pattern of the day placed severe restrictions on the sexual behavior of unmarried persons. Every young person was under pressure to marry. Women had limited education and few job opportunities. Thus marriage accomplished many essential functions:

1. It provided full-time homemakers.
2. It offered career opportunity for women.
3. It assured a family for the unborn.
4. It yielded a needed labor supply.
5. It produced the people needed to populate the wilderness.

WHY MARRY? 19

Far-reaching social, economic, and ideological changes have greatly altered the above functions of married partners. Modern food processing, clothing manufacture, and household appliances have drastically reduced domestic duty. A husband and wife can hold full-time jobs and share housekeeping as a secondary activity. Many modern workers hold full-time employment and do their own housekeeping.

Educational and employment opportunities for women have drastically changed. Women are no longer limited by the necessity to marry and become homemakers. A woman, assured of her ability to be her own breadwinner, has several options: she may enter a career and not marry, she may take a job and marry, or she may change her course from either of the above. She now has options comparable to those which were enjoyed exclusively by men in an earlier era.

The necessity of marriage as a protection for the unborn has been altered by the invention of reliable contraceptives. Couples may use a modern birth-control prescription which allows them to enjoy sexual intercourse without conception.

Modern families are seldom engaged in activities where the parents and children work together to provide the living. Children have ceased to be an economic asset; in fact, families with very few children have a definite financial advantage over larger households. The worldwide emphasis upon reducing population growth has removed the sense of urgency to raise large families.

Sam and Cindy's living-together agreement is remarkably adapted to the reduced functions of the family:

1. Domestic tasks are sideline chores for a couple fully employed elsewhere.
2. Cindy, a graduate of the university, readily found work in a large city.
3. Sam and Cindy were able to enjoy sexual relations fully

without the need to provide a home or family name for children.
4. Two people fully employed and without children have money and time for recreation, travel, or other optional activity.
5. Two young adults who cohabit without bearing children cooperate in the effort to limit population.

WHY GET MARRIED?

The changed role of the family in modern society leads some young adults to ask, "Why marry?" Encouraged by freedom from the necessity of marriage, or concerned over the unhappiness which follows marriage failure, many are choosing to remain single. It was reported in a recent year that the number of households consisting of one person had risen 29% in six years. Singles, including persons widowed or divorced, now make up one-third of all households in America.

Why marry? A complete answer to the question requires further consideration of alternative lifestyles and of the current usefulness of marriage. Is living together without marriage truly desirable? Are the rules about sex for the unmarried out of date or do they still stand as important road signs for behavior? In a time when marriage is widely questioned young people need to find accurate information about sexuality and to equip themselves to make confident choices for their own lives.

Let's Just Live Together

After graduation from high school **John** found a job at a service station. With his first paycheck he rented an apartment and moved in. He and **Sue** were delighted to spend evenings together at the apartment. One night when he took her home, Sue said wistfully, "I wish we didn't have to say good night. It is so wonderful to be together!"

The next evening, the two of them talked about how much fun they could have if they lived together. They knew that their folks would object, but decided that the opportunity was too good to miss. The costs of having an apartment would be the same. They could have a wonderful time together.

The next day Sue packed her suitcase while her parents were at work. Before leaving the house she wrote a note: "I'm going to stay at John's apartment tonight. Please understand us. He and I love each other very much. I love you. Sue."

Sue's parents were deeply troubled. They telephoned at supper time and pleaded with Sue to change her mind. Sue insisted that she was eighteen years of age and had made her decision. She hoped her folks could accept it. She begged them not to worry about her.

After this telephone conversation Sue's mother called their family pastor and asked if he would go to the apartment and talk to Sue and John. The pastor agreed to go.

Living together appears to offer many advantages for persons who are not married. It is pleasant—providing extended companionship and sexual delight. It is simple—free of the complexities of a wedding and the legal entanglements of marriage. It is quick—requiring only enough time to secure shelter and move in. It is economical—a couple may live at lower cost than they could in separate quarters. It is honest—establishing a household is more forthright than secret sex among the unmarried.

At the outset a living-together arrangement looks like a shortcut to happiness. It appears to offer the freedom of single life and the pleasures of marriage without the risks that can attend marriage. In practice, however, it opens a whole new set of problems.

QUESTIONS OF LANGUAGE

Consider first the uncertainty of couples who try to keep their cohabiting secret: Who will answer the telephone? If his relatives try to call him, what will they think when she answers the phone? If her family calls, what will be their response to his voice? The possibility of entertaining comedy rides with a secret cohabitation plan, but the participants are not likely to see the humor.

And there are other delicate questions: Whom will we call if one of us becomes seriously ill? What happens if our parents discover that we are living together? Where will we spend Christmas vacation?

If a couple chooses to inform their family and friends, another set of questions may arise: Will parents continue to assist with college expenses? If not, can we make it on our own? How will we live when we go elsewhere? At a motel? At home? Will we share one room or occupy separate rooms? How shall I introduce my companion?

The latter question has been faced in a variety of ways. One female roommate, finding introductions by her partner embarrassing, adopted the custom of introducing herself before the awkward void engulfed her. Upon arrival or when new persons joined the group, she spoke up with a friendly smile, "Hi! I'm Beth." The people who were meeting her were thus left to guess for themselves who Beth was.

It has been suggested that the use of an extended grunt will convey the needed identification, that is, "This is my uh—friend, Betty."

One effort to fill the language void proposes the title *s'pose* (s'pose they'll get married?).

Barbra Streisand reportedly makes up for our lack of a word designating an unmarried cohabitant by speaking of "my current live-in mate."

SOCIETY'S ATTITUDES

Language inadequacy is of course relatively superficial. Other difficulties in extramarital living together are more serious.

For example, laws in many countries pose formidable problems. The living-together arrangement is illegal in twenty states in America. Penalties range up to three years in prison for persons convicted. Fornication—coitus between the unmarried—is a criminal offense in sixteen states. Few arrests are made, but the laws are on the statute books and might be enforced.

The initial reality which lies behind many problems for unmarried folk living together is society's long-standing disapproval of such arrangements. Our social customs, our language, and our laws presuppose two arrangements for human habitation: a married man and woman live together, or single persons live in "proper" isolation from any possibility of sexual intercourse. Even in an age of widespread freedom to talk about sex and display it in public, public opinion still widely supports this long-standing custom.

Better Homes and Gardens published the results of a current survey of 350,000 readers on the theme, "What's Happening to the American Family?" A magazine spokesman posed the question, "Do you approve or disapprove of two people living together before they get married?" Twenty-six percent voiced approval; 73% reported disapproval.

It is easy for a couple in love to declare that their living arrangements are their own private business, but the involvements of daily life include contacts with a society which may register disapproval in a hundred ways. Unfavorable opinion is most acutely felt in town and rural settings, but even in the environment of a large city or at a major university a household has to deal with myriad people—the plumber, the carpenter, the repairman, the meter reader, the grocer, the policeman, or the neighbor next door. Any one of them may innocently assume marriage and speak of "your husband" or "your wife," address the woman as Mrs. Jones, or otherwise blunder into the couple's "private" arrangements. The opinions of such outsiders are of little consequence in themselves, but to many sensitive persons they are aggravating reminders of guilt.

For generations unmarried folk who cohabited were spoken of as "shacking up" or "living in sin." The latter phrase rated national media coverage early in the Carter administration when the president told a group of government workers, "You people who are living in sin, I hope you'll get married."

One of the most painful consequences of disapproval befell **Henry,** a young engineer who applied to be sent abroad by his company. A routine inquiry preceding the assignment disclosed that Henry lived with **Ruth** but was not married. The company had grave doubts about his suitability to represent them overseas and rejected his application. Henry and Ruth were angry, insisting that their private lives were not company business. Nonetheless, they had no power to reverse the decision.

Whether the company acted justly is a debatable question, but living together unmarried often turns out to be costly in a society which disapproves of the arrangement. Few individuals can live independently in our interrelated social system.

DISAPPOINTING RESULTS

Couples who venture to live together without marital ties also discover that the relationship looks better at the outset than it does as the years pass. Duane Heap, a Presbyterian pastor, served for six years as a volunteer counselor at a mental health clinic. He worked with eleven cohabiting couples who were unmarried. He observed that early interviews reflected happiness and well-being. Couples felt as if they were married. Gradually, insecurity escalated. The women found themselves increasingly nervous. Quarrels grew more serious. Eventually, a devastating argument surfaced: "After all, we're not married." Several complained to the counselor that they were being "used" rather than loved. One couple went to enroll their child in kindergarten and encountered embarrassment in recording the child's legal name, that of the mother. Mr. Heap listened to a rising tide of discontent. Most couples separated. Those who stayed together—two couples—asked him to hear their wedding vows. He reported that initial happiness for most couples turned into disappointment.

The problems of the unmarried frequently appear in the news media. One young mother wrote to Ann Landers:

> Dear Ann: When I was sixteen I moved in with a man who was twenty-five. Everyone assumes Sam and I are married. We now have three children. Sam is crazy about the kids and they adore him. We get along well, except when I mention marriage. Then he says, "We can't. It'll get in the papers and ruin me."
>
> If something should happen to Sam, his sisters and his mother might be entitled to everything he has. I don't want to mention this to Sam because it might look like I'm after his money. Please tell me what to do.
>
> —Worried Sick

Rita, after nine years as the companion and housekeeper for a bachelor friend, wrote to Edwin Roberts, Jr. of the *National Observer:*

> In the beginning, of course, it was just like a honeymoon. We were silly and crazy and happy, and we really appreciated each other. And we were in love and we became more in love—or at least I did. We lived together for nine years. I wanted to get married but Bob would grimace when I suggested it. He said he saw no need for us to be legally tied down.
>
> Then one day it happened. Bob said he had met another girl and he thought they would probably get married. He said he didn't think we should continue to live together under the circumstances, and I said, "Bob, you're absolutely right." And that was that. Nine years down the tube. I gave up nine good, young years when I should have been out circulating and meeting new people. I'll never have any children. I'm just . . . somebody's ex-mistress.

A growing volume of evidence indicates that love has a very poor survival record among unmarried couples. Nancy Moore Clatworthy, associate professor of sociology at Ohio

State University, interviewed forty couples who had lived together and broken up. She heard many complaints.

Often the girls felt they were entitled to more commitment than the boys gave them; they were carrying a heavy load of housework, which with school work limited their outside opportunities severely while their partners continued to enjoy the advantages of freedom, comfort, and pleasure. Girls were restricted in their power to modify the unfair arrangements. One girl said, "He's running around on me! If we were married, I wouldn't put up with it."

Cohabitation frequently caused embarrassing complications in relating to parents. Vacations put severe stress on their friendship. Where could they go and live together?

Dr. Clatworthy concluded her findings with the comment: "Living together creates a whole new set of problems that they wouldn't have had if they had gotten married in the first place."

Joyce Brothers reports a survey which shows that only 30% of the college cohabitants eventually married. Alfred Heasty of the University of Purdue conducted a study of 200 newlywed and dating couples. He reported that the emotional ties between unmarried pairs who had been sleeping together were very similar to the feelings of the married couples. A breakup of such an unmarried pair was "as painful as a divorce."

These local surveys suggest, in the absence of more conclusive research, that living together without marriage is not a very promising venture for an individual who hopes to find enduring love.

THE SOVIET EXPERIENCE

One other area of inquiry may be useful in answering the question, "Why not just live together?" Has any country

28   *LOVE AND LIVING TOGETHER*

attempted to liberalize the traditional custom of marriage?

In a heady burst of enthusiasm after World War I the Soviet Union announced a bold departure from "the restrictions of marriage in the capitalist West." Free love was commended and couples could marry or end a marriage simply by signing appropriate papers. Soviet citizens were encouraged to enjoy their new freedom by rising above the superstitions and unnecessary restrictions of the past. The bold experiment lasted less than two decades.

Michel Gordey, who visited the Soviet Union after World War II, found the government taking "steps toward new marriage patterns for the people's welfare." Gordey spent a day in a people's court and learned that heavy fines were levied on each person who was granted a divorce. Fathers and mothers found it difficult to get a divorce—children required the protection of parents. Gordey was told that the Communist Party "supports the staunch preservation of the family."

A recent visitor to Moscow wrote that Soviet physicians try to dethrone a belief "that premarital intercourse helps to reach full harmony in married life more quickly."

It is curious that a trend toward unmarried cohabitation should appear in many Western countries at a time when Soviet leaders are trying to return to the marital stability they earlier belittled.

SOME OBSERVATIONS

The indications of a high failure rate among those who "just live together" suggest that such informal living arrangements do not satisfy basic human needs. Those needs and ways to satisfy them will be considered in more detail in later chapters.

Some observations are appropriate, however, on the basis of our inquiry up to this point:

1. Sexual intimacy is not in itself an adequate bond to sustain an enduring partnership. The living-together arrangement appears to offer optimum setting for sexual gratification and yet most couples split. Love apparently does not live by sex alone.

2. Enduring love requires more than an agreement to live together "today." People hunger for more security in love. Louise Montague, author and lecturer on marriage and divorce, reported that many youth told her unhappy stories about couples cohabiting without marriage. She explained the results by saying that living-together arrangements are "entered into out of weakness rather than strength, doubt rather than conviction, drift rather than decision." All too often, she concluded, the couples "end up in heartbreak and blasted hopes."

Young people need to look carefully at the seemingly bright prospects for living happily together unwed. Behind the outward appearance of pleasure, convenience, and economy lie many possibilities of disappointment.

What's Wrong with Sex?

Beneath the dispute over whether people should marry or live together unmarried lies a basic disagreement regarding sex. Are there proper and improper relationships between males and females? Western society has long upheld in theory, if not in practice, a code of proper behavior which limits sexual intercourse to marriage. A current wave of opinion insists that the old code has outlived its usefulness. Thus young people are caught in a crossfire of contradictory attitudes.

An unmarried pair who live together soon learn that social disapproval falls specifically upon their violation of the traditional code of sexual behavior.

When her father learned of her new living arrangement, he promptly came for a visit. Getting to the point quickly, he urged, "If you're going to live together, why don't you get married?"

After an exchange of glances between **Sam** and **Cindy,** Sam countered, "Well, you see, Cindy and I don't believe in marriage."

"You don't believe in marriage! You want to enjoy her body without accepting responsibility for her life. If I ever thought one of my girls could get into a mess like this—!"

Sam, choosing his words, replied softly, "What's wrong, Sir, with sex between two people who love each other?"

"If you love each other, why don't you promise to be faithful to one another?"

The argument continued indecisively for hours. When Cindy's

WHAT'S WRONG WITH SEX? 31

father left, his only satisfaction lay in the feeling that he had tried to do his duty to his daughter. Sam and Cindy, reviewing the dispute, agreed that old ideas about sex and marriage were only silly leftovers of a bygone era. Their way, they were convinced, was a new and promising pattern for happiness.

While cohabiting pairs like Sam and Cindy face pressure to conform to tradition, other young people are under fire from the opposite direction.

By the end of her first week in college **Barbara** was greatly confused. Drexel Hall, where she roomed, was one of the University's open dormitories. Her sophomore roommate, **Joanne,** entertained a boyfriend, **Doug,** in the room. Night after night Joanne and Doug visited until late hours. Eventually Barbara, weary from the day's exertion, would change into pajamas in the bathroom, get into bed, and fall asleep.

On Friday night Barbara was restless when she lay down. She was troubled by the constant presence of a dating couple in her room. While lying with her eyes closed she heard a voice whisper from across the room, "Is she asleep yet?" The whispered answer came back, "I think so." Barbara didn't know whether to move and reveal that she wasn't asleep or to lie quietly. Her mind raced to find a solution. Her ears were on sharp alert—mattress bending, vigorous activity, heavy breathing. It was too late to speak!

Through her mind surged a host of questions: Why should she hear the private activity of others? Should she stay up until Doug left each night? What could she do to avoid this embarrassment?

Sounds from the next bed gradually subsided. Barbara recalled that she had been taught to regard sex as something private, and that sex outside marriage was wrong. She remembered **Ben,** her first boyfriend. Those first dates were so exciting! And then—on the fourth date he wanted more intimate affection than she felt free to give. Ben never asked for another

32   LOVE AND LIVING TOGETHER

date. The hurt came back as she remembered it. What is wrong with sex? Why do so many get hurt?

The next afternoon Barbara was still troubled. Joanne came into the room without Doug and said she wanted to talk. She pulled her chair over near Barbara's desk, seated herself and began, "You ought to know, Barbara, if you want a boyfriend here in college you have to get with it! Every boy expects to go to bed with you. It's what this new dormitory arrangement allows. The University Health Service will give you the pill, and you're all set."

Ages seemed to pass before Barbara could speak. Her mind was racing. At orientation the Dean had explained open dorms. He said they offer a "healthier social environment" by giving men and women more freedom to mingle. He had not mentioned Joanne's reason—convenience in going to bed together. Barbara finally found her voice and told Joanne she would think about her suggestion. Joanne hurriedly took off to meet Doug at the library.

Barbara thought again of the day at school when Ben had avoided speaking to her. She remembered how it hurt. Her mother had found her crying in her room and listened sympathetically to the whole story. Mother knew how much Barbara wanted to date, but she stood with Barbara for refusing Ben. Now, under pressure from a college roommate, Barbara wondered what to do. Was Joanne right? Would college men expect to go to bed with any girl they dated? Should she stick to what her parents said about sex? If so, what chance would she have for fun in college?

How do youth find their way through the thicket of contradictory pressures?

A NEW MORALITY?

Advocates of more sexual freedom speak of a new morality, insisting that old ideals have been outdated by modern inventions. The pill and other contraceptives, according to

WHAT'S WRONG WITH SEX? 33

this theory, have put an end to the need for virginity and chastity. Human beings, say the new era prophets, have been liberated from old restraints.

Some insist that traditional sex standards grew from a concern to protect men and the unborn. A virgin bride who was faithful to her husband would bear only his children, thus assuring his posterity. Chastity among the unmarried provided assurance in pre-birth-control ages that the newly-born would have homes that included both a father and a mother. Such rules of conduct, if observed, thus protected a man's right to be sure of his own progeny, and a child's right to a home. Both of these rights, some people insist, can now be safeguarded by the use of contraceptives among the unmarried, thereby rendering the old rules unnecessary.

While modern inventions brought ancient rules about sex into question, society was undergoing a revolution in its attitude toward public discussion of sex. Reticence to allow sex language to be used or the human body to be seen has largely vanished in a great display of everything sexual. Movie stars are filmed going to bed with almost anyone of the opposite sex who strikes their fancy, married or otherwise. Expensive magazines feature nude bodies and encourage a lifestyle centering around the pleasures of sex. A man is supposed to have the power to awaken a woman to sudden, unrestrained desire for his love. A woman's power to turn a man on sexually is supposed to prove her true womanhood.

The uncanny fact about the glamor of sex a la Hollywood or a la Playboy Club is that there is partial truth in the distortion which they peddle, namely, that the physical pleasure of sexual intercourse is a supreme delight. The deception lies in the fact that the same physical relationship can be sordid, distressing, or brutish if the two persons are not joined together by a bond of genuine love.

Much of the public display of sex implies that almost any male and female are equipped to serve one another's sexual desire, as if almost any couple can hop into bed and, if they have the right technique, make each other happy. Sex under these terms is apt to be a rip-off. Each person uses the body of another person to meet his or her own sexual needs.

Influenced by this faulty interpretation of sex, young people may suppose that sex is the primary advantage of marriage and that the marriage certificate is an unrestricted permit to exploit another person's body. Such a concept of marriage leads to the supposition that the benefits of marriage can be found by any male and female who start living together. There is an illusion that delightful sexual pleasure is as easy to turn on as a television set and that intimacy can be ended with the same abruptness.

As a means of offsetting these false images of sex and marriage, several facts should be considered:

1. Performance of the sex act between two strangers may give momentary pleasure, but leave a very distressing emptiness of spirit.

Ralph had always been shy and ill at ease, especially around girls. One night after a round of drinking he resolved to visit a prostitute, hoping to prove to himself that he could overcome his backwardness. When he sobered up the next morning he was so disgusted at his revolting experience that he was sick. He was sure that only someone depraved would go through what he had done. Every time he remembered that night he felt a sharp sense of pain over being such a fool.

2. Sexual intercourse may be extremely unpleasant, even painful, unless a number of human needs are met:
    a) A high level of mutual trust.
    b) Genuine willingness by both partners.
    c) A climate of personal freedom from work and worry.

d) Complete privacy with no chance of intrusion or of being overheard.
e) Good physical health and an absence of undue fatigue by both.
f) A sense of personal well-being, even fun in being together.
g) Freedom from guilt feelings of the wrongness of the experience.

This is only a partial list, but it suggests that happiness in coitus rewards a couple when they are both near the pinnacle of personal joy and well-being. It can easily be seen that much sexual activity, either in or outside marriage, can prove unpleasant or even repulsive. It is unfortunate that the profitable enterprises that glamorize sex fail to demonstrate the wider bond of human love that is necessary for abiding joy.

The impact of public attention to sex is augmented by a variety of peer pressure on youth. Joanne tried to get her roommate Barbara to conform to the sex practices which she had herself accepted. The question may be asked, Who had persuaded Joanne that every college fellow expected his date to go to bed with him?

EXAMINING SLOGANS

Young people, especially those who stand at the beginning of their adult sexual activity, need to examine carefully the slogans which others present:

"Happiness is sexual intimacy." Is it? Who said so? What evidence proves it?

Steve and **Janet** had been dating for several months. Something pleasant was growing between them. One evening they watched another couple leave the dormitory. Both Steve and

Janet knew that the couple had planned an overnight date at a motel. Steve watched Janet for a few moments and then asked, "What do you think of that kind of a date?"

Janet parried, "It's hard to say what's right for them. How does it look to you?"

"I don't think it's a good pattern for us. Two people need to build a very strong bond of love before they go to bed together."

"I thought you might say something like that. You're different from a lot of boys. I have a feeling that I can depend on you."

Both were silent in their own thoughts—one of the pleasures of their easygoing friendship. Janet remembered the tall, athletic boy she dated during her senior year in high school. She liked to be seen with him at dances and games but she was never at ease when they were alone. He kept crowding her for favors— another kiss, much necking and petting. The week before the banquet and prom he told her he was through. He had asked another girl to the prom. That hurt! But now Janet had found a boy who respected her feelings. It was pleasant to be in his arms. She wasn't always playing "defense."

Steve recalled an uncle only three years his senior who had a date almost every night! The exploits the uncle told about had made Steve uneasy: What if you're caught? What if she becomes pregnant? His uncle had easy answers for every question, but that quacky remedy for pregnancy sounded dangerous. What did the girl think of all this? Were dates so important to her that she accepted intercourse every night?

Steve had watched his uncle's problems pile up: grades dropping from honor roll to borderline or failure, endless quarrels with his parents, debts for gas and tires, never enough sleep! Steve could never quite put his thinking all together, but he decided to take a long hard look at sex before he let his own life get messed up.

"Happiness is sexual intimacy." Is it? Maybe so. Maybe not.

"Everybody's doing it." Are they? And even if many are

doing it, why should I? Is right decided by what everybody else does?

There is a widespread belief that sexual intercourse is much more common among the unmarried than it was in earlier ages. Is this belief supported by reliable evidence? Only limited surveys have been made and their accuracy is not easy to verify.

Dr. and Mrs. Daniel Offer, a psychiatry and social research team at Michael Reese Hospital in Chicago, spent eight years interviewing sixty-one teenage boys. They found that only half of their test group had experienced sexual intercourse by the time they were three years beyond high school graduation. Those who had not engaged in sexual intercourse gave various explanations: "fear of the experience," "too busy to spend time with girls," "no need to indulge," or "there's plenty of time in the future for sexual involvement."

More than twenty-two thousand youth responded to a "Who's Who Among American High Students" survey. Seventy-one percent said they had not engaged in premarital sex.

Apart from the survey, there are indications that many youth do not even date. A comparison of any school class list with attendance at a school dance makes the planning committee wonder if their work went unappreciated. Observers report that large numbers of college men and women sit in their rooms or go out with a group of their own sex on date nights.

The slogan "Everybody's doing it" deserves thoughtful attention. There is considerable evidence that the sexual revolution is more real in talk than in deeds. Ira L. Reiss, in an article summarizing his research on sexual behavior, asserted: "The popular notion that America is undergoing a sexual 'revolution' is a myth." His findings indicated a major shift in attitudes but not in behavior.

Even if the belief is accurate, if youth en masse are involved in more sexual activity before marriage, there is still reason to inquire, Is that course of action desirable for me? Someone playfully imagined a conversation between two pigs in the ancient story about a herd of three thousand swine rushing toward a precipice. One pig said, "Where in the world are we going?" "I don't know," said a second pig, running at full speed, "but we're sure getting there in a hurry!"

Any youth in our society who feels the need to do what others are doing faces great confusion. Contradictory examples of behavior are widely available. If a young person is uncomfortable under group pressure in one crowd, he or she can probably find other social groups which think and act differently. Personal decisions about behavior need to be made by each individual. When someone says, "Everybody's doing it," thoughtful youth may wisely reply, "Oh, is that so? I guess I'll make my own choices as I think best."

"You need sex to grow up, to cure acne, etc." Who says you do? What evidence is there?

Sexual intercourse is, for most people, one of the experiences of maturing. Youth understandably want to hurry into the full privileges of adult life. But does coitus speed a person toward healthy maturation? Obviously not. One college dean after many years of counseling with students observed that the more promiscuous students he had known were usually the least mature. An obsessive interest in sex often pointed to serious emotional instability.

"The pill sets us free from the old rules." Does it?

WHAT'S WRONG WITH SEX?

The pill itself is considered to be highly effective in preventing pregnancy if it is taken according to instructions. However, the woman involved needs to keep precise records on her own menstrual cycle and to take the pill daily for a prescribed number of days. If she omits the pill in the prescribed interval and engages in sexual intercourse, pregnancy is an ever-present possibility. Unmarried persons who cohabit have no automatic assurance that they will remain childless.

The pill, incidentally, does nothing to prevent venereal disease. The old rule of chastity outside marriage continues to be the surest way to avoid infection. Throughout the world gonorrhea and syphilis have spread in our age to "epidemic proportions." In one recent year there were an estimated three million new cases of gonorrhea in America alone. Modern marriage laws generally require blood tests prior to marriage, thus protecting spouses and their offspring from these ravaging ailments. The unmarried ordinarily have no protection. If anyone tells you that the old rules about sex no longer apply, you need not be deceived. The pill and modern drugs provide partial freedom from old fears, but the biological realities of conception and venereal infection have not changed.

Young people need to check out the many myths which pass for facts in the realm of sex. Human beings mature through a broad range of types of experience, a process which is neither speeded by sexual intercourse nor delayed by chastity.

"What's wrong with sex?" a young person asks.

"Nothing," comes the answer of an older friend, "nothing is wrong with sex itself. Sex is a great boon to the human race. But, sex misused—sex exploited—is a tragic source of grief and disappointment. Our society places youth in a crossfire of contradictory advice. Anyone who wants to emerge safely from such a no-man's-land needs to think carefully, 'Who am I? What is right for me?'"

Some couples make a deliberate choice to wait for the fulfillment of their love on their honeymoon. Their reasoning is like that of the children who were told where their parents had hidden the Christmas presents and were then given the choice—to peek ahead of time or to wait until Christmas. The children in that family decided to save the pleasure of finding and opening their gifts until the best time and place—Christmas morning beside the tree.

What Do You Really Want?

About nine-thirty yesterday evening (according to a campus counselor's notebook) my telephone rang. The caller identified herself as a student in a university dormitory. She said she remembered my saying a few weeks earlier that I could come during off-duty hours to talk with any student in difficulty. She said that a girl down the hall was in some desperate trouble. The girl stayed in her room and cried most of the time. She couldn't eat, she couldn't sleep, and she couldn't study either. She and her boyfriend had said that they would like to have a chance to talk with me.

Fifteen minutes later I met the couple in front of the dormitory and we drove to a truck stop at the edge of the city where people were coming and going and where high booths would allow us to sit and talk without being overheard. We sat down together, the two of them obviously anxious. **Winton,** an attractive boy, opened the conversation: "**Annette** and I love each other, but we are in deep trouble." Annette, who was sobbing by this time, added, "I am two weeks late and I don't know what to do. I would rather die than tell my parents that this has happened."

With much crying on her part and much concern on his part they talked about their predicament and what to do. They did not have the income to marry but they were desperate for lack of any other alternative. Neither of them wanted to tell her parents.

I suggested that Annette consult a physician to determine whether or not she was pregnant. This suggestion brought signs of relief to both their faces. Then we explored what to do if the physician reported that a baby was to be expected. I suggested that we talk again after the appointment with the doctor.

42 LOVE AND LIVING TOGETHER

I drove them back to the dormitory. Winton went with Annette to the entrance and then came back to ride with me to his dormitory. On the way he told me about how for years he had been living to have fun in any way that he could. It had never mattered what he did or how he behaved himself with any other girl. But he said earnestly, "Annette is different. She is very special in my life and I don't want to lose her." He talked at length about the agony he had brought her. We reviewed alternative ways to solve the problem and parted about midnight.

This morning the student who had originally called me phoned to say, "Thank you very much for helping my friends last night. Annette came in more calm than she has been for days. She told me what she was going to do and I helped her get the name and the phone number of a physician. She went to bed and slept soundly. This morning she awakened in pain and came running to tell me that her nightmare was over—her period had begun." The student thanked me again and I assured her I was glad to help.

(From the same notebook six weeks later) I hear that the two students I saw at night several weeks ago are not dating. Winton is deeply upset, but Annette refuses to see him. She says she is not free and happy in his presence any more. The love-trust relationship between them has been broken.

Winton lost the girl who seemed to fulfill his hopes for a life partner because he thoughtlessly pursued the short-term pleasures of sex. Annette's love was crushed by the realization that she could not rely on him to consider her needs. She had allowed herself to enjoy his affection, wanting to please him at any cost. Their painful ordeal destroyed the love that was growing between them. Behavior that grows from physical desires may obliterate a person's cherished hopes for the future.

Can powerful physical yearnings be handled to assure lasting happiness? Should young adults postpone their yearnings for sexual pleasure in order to attain long-range goals? Does such self-control contribute to enduring happiness later on?

SETTING LONG-RANGE GOALS

Each unmarried individual can wisely review his or her long-range goals and weigh them against the desire for instant pleasure. Several questions need to be honestly faced:

Is sexual gratification a priority? There is no question that the urge for sexual fulfillment is insistent and powerful. Stimulants that arouse that urge are conspicuously present. Many men read literature generously illustrated with nude or nearly nude women. Similar magazines display pictures of nude men. Dormitory rooms are often replete with suggestive posters. Styles of clothing for both men and women accent sexuality. Necking and petting arouse seemingly irresistible desire. Can healthy people be expected to resist such pressure?

The traditional answer has been yes. Religious orders that teach chastity as a lifetime discipline recommend a process called sublimation, diverting energy into other useful endeavor. Ordinary individuals discover a variety of ways to master their own desires: cultivation of wide-ranging interests in reading, vigorous physical exercise, and avoiding the stimulants which deliberately evoke passion for sex.

Control can be established if an individual is convinced that sexual pleasure should be subordinate to more important, long-range goals. The question faces each individual: Is sexual satisfaction a priority goal? If the answer is no, then appropriate daily routines need to be maintained to use energy in other activities.

Is lasting companionship your aim? Are you satisfied to play the field as a single person? Is it enough to establish a living-together arrangement that allows day-to-day companionship? Or do you really hope to find one person whom you love and trust as a lifetime companion?

If security and familiarity are important to you, you need to rate highly a lifestyle that provides lasting companionship.

Do you want a home with children? Have you dreamed throughout your growing years of becoming a parent? Do you want to have offspring? Do you yearn to play with your own little boy or girl and to watch them learn and grow?

If a family is one of your fond dreams, then choose carefully the course which will enable you to see your dreams come true.

MARRIAGE AND UNMARRIAGE

How do marriage and living together unmarried compare in providing for the attainment of the above goals? Someone may quickly answer that neither arrangement guarantees any of the goals. With one divorce for every three marriages, no one can deny the disappointed hopes of many who marry.

Jerry Lewis once said that after he was married he came to value one wedding gift especially—a movie of the wedding. He said he could mount it on the movie projector, run it through backwards, and come out a free man.

Many marriages fail to yield the measure of happiness that couples expect. But how do the satisfactions of unmarried living together compare?

The ideal of marriage is a growing unity between a man

and a woman wherein their hearts, minds, and bodies merge and mutually support one another. The process occurs ideally over a period of many months, perhaps even a year or more, before it is formally established. The wedding ceremony is a public event allowing two people to confirm to one another the greatest gift exchange of all—the gift of their lives to one another. In the ceremony each person essentially says, "I give myself to you, to love and serve you as long as we live."

The bride and groom, knowing the frailty and unpredictability of any human intention, seek the blessing of God and the prayers and good wishes of a surrounding company of loved ones and friends. In marrying, the couple and the witnesses establish a supportive arrangement—personal, social, legal, and ecclesiastical—to strengthen the bond that joins two lives.

From their wedding onward they enjoy hearty social approval in living together. Their sexual activity is their own private experience, but all who know that they live together wish them the highest pleasure. The inhibitions of years of training are swept away and a couple are free to share their joy without any embarrassing reproach. They have words that define their relationship—*husband* and *wife*. They are received in public with honor and have a shared surname for honest and lawful identity. Each year the circle of loved ones and friends may celebrate the anniversary of the wedding day.

In the months and years that follow, the oneness of mind and spirit often continues to grow. Many couples who celebrate their silver and golden wedding anniversaries assert that their love has deepened and their pleasure together has grown with the passing years.

When crises develop between spouses, they have a mutual pledge of loyalty to each other that reinforces their efforts to adjust to one another. Often a friend or relative, a pastor or other counselor, assists them to talk through their disagreements and renew their happiness. Couples who actively participate in a church find a wide circle of supportive friends to stabilize their marriage when anger threatens to fracture their oneness.

By contrast, the living-together arrangement has very little to support its continuance aside from the affection of two people. Either party is free to withdraw any day. There can be no planning for a future and no lawful begetting of children. The couple even encounter difficulty in the purchase of a home or in buying insurance. Neither partner gives any promise of loyalty. No surrounding circle of family and friends can defend their togetherness. Any passing flirtation attractive to either party can terminate the arrangement. Any disagreement may lead to separation.

Long-range goals of companionship and the establishment of a home and family fare poorly for a couple who prefer to make no binding commitments to one another.

What happens to people involved in such an arrangement for living together?

Men whose needs are satisfied in day-to-day companionship do fairly well. They have domestic convenience, sexual pleasure, and maximum freedom. If one woman becomes unsatisfactory, the man can usually find another one, often much younger than himself. Even if he eventually hopes to marry and have children, he has no cause to be in a hurry. Men can normally procreate as long as they have normal health, approximately from ages fourteen to seventy-three.

Women in the short run find much satisfaction—companionship, financial support, and affection. However, their insecurity is almost certain to multiply any way the unmarriage proceeds. If the couple refrains from begetting children, she may forfeit her chance to bear children at all. A woman's years of fertility rarely extend beyond age forty-five. Her desirability to other men likewise runs down as years pass. Social custom seldom allows her to find a younger mate, further reducing her chances of having another companion. Thus instead of preventing injustice experienced by women in marriage, the living-together arrangement spawns greater likelihood of injustice to women. An unwed woman who cohabits has neither marriage nor equal leverage to influence the conduct of her companion.

Children fare worst of all. The child of an unmarried couple is classified as "illegitimate." Children are called names and are embarrassed at school. The stigma of society's disapproval is likely to fall with heaviest impact upon the offspring, who had no voice in deciding the living arrangements of the parents.

Some may quickly object that most of the unhappy consequences of unmarriage are the fault of a rigid and unjust society. There may be a large element of truth in this objection, but that fact does not remove the harsh results. Social changes do take place and some changes are occurring, but the process is slow, and the pioneers of new living arrangements may find that the changes they seek never occur.

A couple who want to share enduring love are wise to seek marriage as the best supporting arrangement currently available. Each person needs to study what he or she wants in life. Some, at least temporarily, may be like Sam and Cindy, happy not to be married, preferring not to have children, and glad to have day-to-day pleasure in being together. Only time will reveal how long their arrangement will satisfy their needs.

For most individuals, a careful review of life goals will point toward restraint in present sexual indulgence in order to enhance the prospects of happiness in marriage.

What Is Love?

Charlotte and **Jim** sat across the desk from **Pastor Jones,** answering questions for a marriage information sheet. The inquiry shifted from name, address, and age to items of marriage readiness. The pastor posed his next question: "Charlotte, what reasons lead you to think that you and Jim will be happy in marriage?"

"We love each other. It's as simple and wonderful as that!"

"Jim, do you want to add another reason or reasons?"

"No, Sir. That is our reason. Three months ago we had no idea about anything like this. In fact, we didn't think we liked each other."

Jim laughed and glanced at Charlotte who, sharing his laughter, added, "One night we were at a party where we both went to the kitchen to volunteer in serving refreshments. When we realized that we had come separately to make the same offer, we laughed and our eyes met in a new way. Jim broke the spell by suggesting to the hostess, 'Maybe you can use both of us.' She accepted us and told us what to do. While we went our ways to serve we were eager to return and be close to one another. After the refreshments had been served we found a table and visited for the rest of the evening."

"Here we are three months later," said Jim. "What a world of happenings in three months! We've bought a house, have it partly furnished, and have set a wedding date—that is, if it suits you. We never believed love would strike us like this."

Six months after the wedding, Jim telephoned the pastor:

"Charlotte and I would like to talk to you. You said after our wedding that you would be glad to help us if we ran into trouble. Well, we need to talk to you."

The pastor called at the home and found that their love was floundering among a host of irritating differences. Charlotte was comfortable sleeping with one blanket when Jim needed two blankets. Jim squeezed the toothpaste tube in the middle and Charlotte rolled it from the end. The magic of their sudden love and hasty courtship had vanished. They laughed in embarrassment over their differences, but they were glad to explore possible ways to reduce friction and recover the thrill of their earlier love.

ROMANTIC LOVE

Jim and Charlotte originally gave love as their one and only reason to expect to be happily married. They let feelings of love hasten them into wedlock when they were not even well-acquainted.

Young people growing up have frequent exposure to glamorized love, romantic love, on stage, page, and screen. Love strikes like a thunderbolt from the skies. Nobody can predict it and nobody can defy its power. Everyone who is old enough to be hit by such sudden "love" needs to acquire enough information to know that the thunderbolt may be *infatuation*, that is, literally, a "filling into" a person of "foolishness." A romantic infatuation may race into the heavens like a skyrocket on the fourth of July, explode into beautiful and brilliant patterns, and fall to earth almost unseen.

Such passionate romance probably testifies more to the prior loneliness of the two persons than to their informed affection for one another. The major peril of thunderbolt love lies in the fact that a male and female may find erotic excitement together who are poorly matched for an enduring love affair. A whirlwind courtship may be the forerunner of a marital tornado.

Young people learn to dream about "falling in love" or of being the one with whom someone else "falls in love." The dangerous myth includes the supposition that there is one particular person somewhere who will be *the* one. The sudden emergence of romance, it is supposed, is full evidence that the right person has now appeared, and that a person so smitten by love should accept these signs as reliable indicators of love and let the romance grow. Presumably love is as irresistible as a case of the chicken pox.

In contrast to these modern ideas, ancient societies attached little importance to love as a precondition of marriage. For example, Near Eastern families in the era of the Bible's origin exercised great care in the choosing of marriage partners for their youth. The parents considered age, background, disposition of the individuals, health, appearance, work interest, and the woman's skills as a homemaker. The families negotiated with one another and jointly scheduled the wedding. It was assumed that a man and woman properly matched would learn to love one another after the wedding.

In the past two centuries in western European society we have arrived at a concept that youth should choose their own mates and that love between them should precede a decision to marry. We have allowed a great deal more intermingling of boys and girls in their growing years and have largely entrusted to them the responsibility for making a wise choice of a life partner. There is reason to believe, however, that the myths about romantic love seriously interfere with the ability of youth to select a mate wisely. It further hampers marital adjustment because it leads youth to expect continued euphoric bliss.

WHAT KIND OF LOVE?

Any young person who thinks that he or she is in love needs to ask some very serious questions: What kind of love am I experiencing? Is it infatuation? Is it physical attraction? Is biological urge drawing me to this other person, or do we also discover that we are kindred spirits with a growing unity of heart and mind between us? Does my love lead me to want to seek the other person's happiness above all else? Does it make me want to give myself fully for that person's well-being?

To assure a larger measure of happiness in marriage we need really to clarify the true nature of love.

The pastor's discussion with Jim and Charlotte began with irritations which could be resolved by accommodation to one another. Pastor Jones asked, "Have you considered twin beds? Many couples find that they sleep much better in separate beds. Going to one another's bed is part of the fun."

Charlotte nodded thoughtfully, then stood abruptly. "Oh, I made some lemonade and almost forgot. Would you like a glass?"

"Sounds great! Thank you."

When Charlotte reached the kitchen, Jim said hesitantly, "I think our most serious problem is not our double bed. It's sex. When I'm with her I'm ready for intercourse almost anytime, but she usually doesn't want me. Is something wrong with me?"

"Maybe you turn on faster than she does."

"What can I do?"

Charlotte returned with a tray of glasses, served the two men, and seated herself with her own glass. Jim reopened the conversation.

"I told Pastor Jones about our troubles in bed."

Charlotte spoke earnestly: "I don't know what is wrong with me. Before we were married we spent many hours in each other's arms. I used to yearn to be all his. Now, with my job all day and work here all evening, I'm tired at bedtime."

WHAT IS LOVE? 53

Turning toward Jim, she continued, "You watch TV or read! When I get through with my work, I've had it. And intercourse seems awful!"

The pastor, looking toward Jim, reflected, "Before your wedding Charlotte wanted you, Jim. You held her in your arms. You visited with her. You gave her enough time to want to be closer to you."

"I begin to see it now," Jim ventured. "I'm all steamed up when she only wants to be held and caressed! But how can we find time? She's always got work to do! Maybe, if I help her . . ."

"I'd like that," said Charlotte. "I haven't wanted to say it, but I work away from home every day and I've been feeling cheated when I have so much work at home. We ought to have equal duty at home, Honey."

"I'm willing to try," Jim responded. "I had no idea you felt that way. I just thought you were more eager to clean the kitchen than to be with me."

The conversation closed with a discussion of possibilities to share housework and find more time together watching TV or visiting.

About a month later Pastor Jones heard Jim call to him on the street in front of the post office: "Hi! I've wanted to thank you for coming out to see us."

"I was glad to come. How is it going?"

"Not right yet, but better! We've decided that love is *all day long*. We do as much as we can together. I even enjoy scraping the dirty dishes while she loads the dishwasher. Charlotte seems better . . . able to have fun. We talk more. We don't quarrel the way we did. And we're finding more pleasure in bed!"

"You're working it out together. I'm happy for you. God bless you."

Jim proceeded into the post office while the pastor headed for his car. Through his mind passed Jim's words: "Love is *all day long*."

When he reached his study Pastor Jones found his mind absorbed by thoughts of Jim and Charlotte. He decided to send his thinking to them by letter:

Dear Jim and Charlotte,

I was delighted to see Jim a few minutes ago and to hear of your progress in understanding one another. You have made an important discovery. "Love *is* all day long."

You may have discovered that your hours at the table are exceedingly important for love-renewing. Don't be misled. I'm not suggesting that meals be turned into necking parties. There are ways to express affection at the table, but I mean more than that. Mealtime is telling time—personal concerns, joys, and the needs of friends can be discussed. The meal hour is also planning time—when to expect the other home, what the evening will hold, and scheduled events in days to come. Thoughtful sharing and thorough communication renew the unity you have in love.

Many couples include prayer before meals. Devotions turn your being together into a private sacrament of love and thanksgiving. I commend this idea to you. If your life together at the table is healthy, you will find joy as you celebrate your love in bed.

May true love grow in your lives through many years.

Sincerely,
J. W. Jones

SELF-GIVING LOVE

One of the most distinctive contributions of the Christian gospel is its definition of love. Jesus of Nazareth taught love of God and neighbor as the central motif of life. The love he urged his followers to live is responsible and intelligent self-giving. It manifests concern to help the wounded, kindness to the accused, and friendship with the outcast. Such love has only incidental relationship to romance. A couple who love each other in this deeper, broader way find life by losing self for the sake of the other. In his famous hymn to love (1 Cor. 13) the Apostle Paul wrote that love "endures all things." Such love may even lose itself for the sake of another person.

Paul and **Jan** dated for almost two years in college. Their joy together enlivened every day. They understood one another and were mutually helpful in schoolwork and in resolving difficulties. Only one shadow fell across their friendship: Jan planned to become a dentist and Paul was aiming for a doctorate in psychology. Both anticipated years of graduate study before marriage was feasible. Neither of them would ask the other to postpone or cancel a career dream in order to marry. Out of mutual regard and with a severe sense of loss they agreed to separate. Through the years of graduate study they remembered one another fondly, both hoping that the time might come when they could come together again. They each loved selflessly enough to lose the other for the other's sake.

Self-giving love may even rise above long-standing disappointment. Masters and Johnson, well-known sex therapists, report the experience of a couple who had been married thirty years when they came to a sex therapy clinic. Group conversation disclosed two facts: they loved each other with deep and tender affection, and continued to do so despite thirty years of unsatisfactory sexual relations. The therapy clinic greatly enhanced their love by helping them to add joy through newly discovered sexual harmony. They had loved each other enough to be loyal in spite of unsatisfactory sexual relations.

A couple who feel "swept off their feet" in romance need to consider also this deeper self-giving love. The noted author C. S. Lewis likened love between two people to a violin and a bow. Used together by a skilled musician the two separate instruments emit beauty of sound that no one could imagine by viewing them unused. When a man and woman grow together into oneness of mind and heart, the beauty of their love is a source of great joy. Such love is intelligent and responsible self-giving. It yields rewarding unity to those who share it.

Able to Love

The trouble in the Garden of Eden did not begin with the apple in the tree but with the pair on the ground. According to the Bible story in Genesis 2–3, the human race began in tragicomedy. The woman was beguiled to eat the forbidden fruit and she persuaded the man to eat of it. Thereafter they both felt guilty and tried to clothe themselves with leaves and to hide among the bushes.

When they had been found, the man blamed the woman, and she accused the serpent. They were subsequently evicted from their first home. Later one of their sons in a fit of jealous rage killed his brother. The ancient story records no affection among the members of the first human family. Apparently humanity began to make history without being able to love.

No member of that original family intended to bring tragedy upon themselves—each individual simply acted in his own selfish interest. They lived in a materially bountiful garden without the ability to think and act unitedly.

NATURAL OR LEARNED?

The modern myth of romantic love includes the idea that loving is natural, something given in the way we are made. There is of course an element of truth in such thinking. We are equipped to experience a powerful attraction to the opposite sex. We generally have a deep yearning not to be alone. We long for companionship, to be with another person whom we trust. Loving is natural.

However, hatred is also natural, and selfishness is as fundamental to human nature as self-giving. From the very hour of birth an infant rends the air with cries for food and comfort. When needs are not quickly met the cries grow louder and more insistent. Thus at a very early age, the child knows how to dominate others for personal benefit. As years pass, children display amazing skill in controlling and exploiting others. This selfish strategy of a child usually includes resistance to serving others. Thus it is quite natural for a person to avoid responsibility and to resist any role of subservience. Many of the difficulties which people confront in living together originate in natural tendencies to control and use other people.

Individuals who live together unmarried often display a serious deficiency of intelligent and responsible concern for their partners. Many living-together arrangements are founded upon such propositions as the following:

"I enjoy the pleasure of your affection, so I love you today."

"I do not know if I will love you tomorrow, so I make no promises."

"I want to be free to do as I please."

"We cannot afford to be married yet, but we love each other."

Obviously, such statements reveal a will for self-gratification coupled with a denial of responsibility for continuing care of the person "loved." It is logical to ask if the affection affirmed is truly love. Any individual involved in such limited "love" is likely to begin to think about certain questions:

"If I become ill, will my partner stay around?"

58   LOVE AND LIVING TOGETHER

"If my live-in mate loves me so much today, why does he/she refuse to accept responsibility for my well-being tomorrow?"

"Can we never plan for our lives beyond today? What about a home? children? our future?"

John and **Sue** were thrilled when she moved to his apartment. It seemed a very natural way to act when they loved each other so much. They could not afford a home and children yet, but they could enjoy living together for the time being.

Sue's pastor called at John's apartment about nine o'clock that evening. Sue was embarrassed by his coming, but invited him to come in. She and John explained that their love had led them to try living together. The pastor acknowledged that they were very much in love.

John entered the conversation to explain the advantages of not being married: "We've made no promises, so if we split no one is hurt."

"As I understand it, you agree to live together but you keep the door open so you can leave at any time."

"Yes, Sir, that is what we have agreed upon. Sue is free and I am free."

"Such love is very different from the love of a married couple. My wife and I promised to stay together and our promises help us to be strong in our love. You have no promises to help you to keep on loving."

Sue responded thoughtfully, "When I moved here this afternoon I thought this was just like getting married, but it really isn't. I love you, John, and I really want our love to have a strong future."

After further conversation about living together married or unmarried, the pastor suggested that they think together about their future. He invited them to let him know if they wanted to talk with him again, and excused himself.

The next morning Sue's mother called the pastor and asked,

"What did you do? Sue came home last night. She said she and John had changed their minds after your visit."

"I only helped them think through the difference between marriage and the way they were beginning to live together. I know that Sue was thinking seriously when I left, but I did not know what they would decide to do."

The living-together arrangement is often an expression of an unreadiness for abiding love. Many couples—the married as well as the unmarried—are unsuccessful in living together because they are unable to love. Romantic love between a man and a woman may come easily, quickly, and naturally, but if even one of them lacks the ability to love in the deeper, broader way that we have been considering, the continuation of romantic love is highly unlikely. If people could rub a magic lamp, utter a secret formula, and receive instantly what was asked, many would seek the ability to love.

THE ABILITY TO LOVE

There is no magic process for creating true love, but we may be able to grow in our ability to love if we analyze the essential nature of loving. Three areas need to be brought into clearer focus:

Self-love. It is popularly assumed that a loving person needs to be completely devoid of self-love. However, this idea needs to be carefully examined. A person with low self-esteem is ill-equipped to love anyone else. Such a person is often driven by an intense need to dominate others and to scorn any act of service on their behalf. Such a willful, domineering individual arouses hostility in others. Experiencing rejection, a self-centered person often develops an obsessive urge to prove self-worth by outstripping all others in getting wealth, prestige, fame, or knowledge. Success in such a feverish quest to prove worth is likely to cause even greater estrangement and loneliness. There is profound truth in the ancient commandment, "You shall love your neighbor *as yourself*."

A sensible regard for oneself is the foundation of personal maturity and of the ability to love someone else. Healthy self-love enables a person to act with confidence, to rise above self-concern and relate to others.

Many young people in the teen years are painfully self-conscious. They blush and have difficulty speaking to youth of the opposite sex or to a stranger. This widespread difficulty may be traced to uncertainty about self-worth: "Am I unattractive? Do others consider me a stupid kid? Or do they approve of me?"

In the process of growing to maturity such self-questioning is usually reduced to a level where it is little or no hindrance. This happens most often in one of two ways.

The first way is self-acceptance. A youth may gradually or suddenly come to realize that doubts of self-worth lessen effectiveness. Therefore there is no advantage in continually worrying about what someone else thinks. The awakening may come in thoughts such as these: "I am what I am. I cannot change and be somebody else. I am ready to do what I can do and quit wasting my energy worrying about what others think about me. I shall set my thoughts and efforts on my work or play and let self-conscious doubts fall by the wayside."

The other way to overcome painful self-consciousness lies in successful effort. Most parents heartily approve of a youth who fulfills his or her responsibility. Teachers and coaches usually heap approval on the student who does well. The young person who accepts self and concentrates on behavior that wins approval discovers growing awareness of personal worth.

The importance of a healthy sense of self-worth for success in living together must not be overlooked. The foundation of the ability to love is laid through many years in the emerging self-image of a child or youth. A review of this process is appropriate.

Healthy self-esteem begins early in life. Adequate food, plenty of sleep, continuous loving care, and ample conversation convey to the infant an awareness of self-worth. Prompt attention to hunger or discomfort fosters a sense of security. Varied adventures from early childhood onward convey to the person either a good feeling or a sense of fear and of little worth.

A youth with healthy self-awareness finds a job, does it well, and advances toward the ability to earn a living. The young person who has proved successful in work is motivated to assume responsibility for health, clothing, and daily routines of eating and sleeping. He or she, through growing self-confidence, qualifies to become independent of the support and authority of parents.

Emotional stability flowers with the development of self-support and self-control. One of the hazards of adolescence today lies in the growing hiatus between the time when one attains the physical capacity of an adult and the age when one achieves economic independence. Children in the modern era generally consume so much protein that the average age of puberty has dropped from seventeen to thirteen years. Meanwhile the age when schooling ends and self-support begins has been raised from as early as twelve to a range of nineteen to twenty-six years, depending upon educational requirements. In this span of years, approximately thirteen to twenty-one, young people are expected to maintain Spartan self-control sexually and to continue to be subject to parental authority. Obviously a youth needs a generous measure of self-love to make a happy passage through the adolescent years.

Furthermore powerful affection is often felt before the boy or girl is old enough *to continue* to love another person.

> At sixteen years of age **Carol** was madly in love with **Mike.** At seventeen, after a painful breakup with Mike, she thought her future looked rosy with **Phil.** At twenty-two Carol was engaged to **Joe,** whom she had dated for over two years. She said, "It's so different this time. Joe and I really know each other. We have finished our schooling. As soon as he finds a suitable job, we can set a wedding date. Those other love affairs could never have lasted."

Intelligent and mature self-love enables a person to love another person on an enduring basis. An individual who desires to gain the ability to love needs to appreciate the value of a healthy love for self.

Love for others. The ancient commandment which referred to self-love was really aimed at love for the neighbor—love toward another person. As a person acquires an inner sense of self-worth he or she quietly learns a genuine regard for others. A confident person can turn off the clamor of self-centered thought and be attentive to someone else.

An intelligent awareness of others demonstrates itself in wide varieties of interaction: What do the people around me want? What do my parents expect of me? Why is a teammate so scornful? What troubles flood the mind of my cranky teacher? Why is my brother or my roommate so moody and prone to explosions of temper?

When a person turns toward other people with a sensitive concern for their well-being the art of loving becomes a practical possibility.

Skills in loving. The art of loving is like a hidden treasure which many seek. Reports of its whereabouts spread far and wide, but only a limited number ever come upon the secret way that enables them to find it.

Some make the happy discovery early in life that loving is essentially a matter of giving. A child draws a picture for mother at the church school on Sunday morning. Presenting the gift is a thrilling event. If mother is alert and rewards the giver with a smile and a loving caress, she awakens new possibilities of happiness. The drawing will be followed by many other drawings, by flowers crudely picked, or by a glass of water held forth in a tiny hand. A child who discovers the joy of presenting a gift grows attentive to what others appreciate—helping with the grocery sacks, running an errand, or giving words of encouragement.

Instruction in the art of loving does not begin with explanations about the birds and the bees but with simple acts of self-giving—to care, to help, to touch, to hold, to kiss, or to share. A child who learns to devote his or her thought to others continues to practice the art of loving through intelligent and generous words and deeds.

The skills of loving can be refined by practice—careful observation, thoughtful inquiry, genuine attentiveness, generous appreciation, and eager helpfulness. Through the practice of these skills many people build a surrounding climate of kindness.

Consider the skill of thoughtful inquiry: "Have I offended you? I did not intend to do so." Such a question may soften the hostility of a co-worker or a superior.

In the practice of loving, simple words sincerely spoken are extremely fruitful. A couple who wish to enrich their love need to make frequent use of a few basic expressions:

"Thank you, Dear."
"You're welcome!"
"I'm sorry."
"That's all right."
"I love you."

SEX AND LOVE

Thus far our consideration of the ability to love has not included sex, or any of the sex-related activities usually associated with love. The omission has been deliberate because one popular idea of love is sex-oriented—a male and female "love" each other as an outgrowth of sexual attraction. If a husband and wife are unhappy, friends may guess that they are not well-adjusted sexually. Better techniques of foreplay and intercourse are recommended. Such ideas grow out of a strange confusion over reality.

In fact, love is a basic trust and affection which is shared in every joint activity of the day. A couple who are at odds over authority, money, or children are unlikely to find happiness through intercourse, while a pair who enjoy unity of heart and mind can usually find happiness in the intimacy of their bed.

What is the relationship of sex to loving? Sex offers a superb way for a man and woman to express their devotion to one another and to celebrate joyfully their essential oneness. Through caressing, kissing, and embracing, they convey tender affection for one another. Given a setting of freedom, good fun, and physical well-being, such expressions of love build to a climax of supreme delight in sexual intercourse. Probably the highest pleasure persons ever know is the gift which partners bring to each other in sexual fulfillment. Sex needs to be understood in this way: It adds special beauty to the experience of a couple who cherish one another. It is one of the best expressions of a love which is founded in mutual trust and helpfulness.

Loving is not a simple art, nor is it merely cosmetic—putting a pretty cover over an ordinary or ugly reality. Loving begins in a healthy awareness of self. It extends to a genuine concern for others, and it flowers into the skills of giving self for others. Married lovers find that sexual intercourse enables them to give each other joy that is ecstatic. There is no shortcut to enduring happiness of this quality. Loving thoughtfulness and action on behalf of another person opens the way for two lives to be joined as one. In some sense the physical union which is a mutually happy experience represents a supreme attainment of unity in the whole range of living together.

TESTING YOUR ABILITY

Are you able to love another person in a way that will enable you to find enduring happiness? You can test yourself with the following questions:

1. Do I get along well with my parents?
2. Do I work and play harmoniously with my brothers and sisters?
3. Do I have a few good friends?
4. Do I have a wider circle of friends of both sexes?
5. Have I one or more trusted persons with whom I can discuss anything that troubles me?

If you find yourself saying no to any of these questions, you may need to review your attitudes and actions toward others and reconsider your own ability to love. You may think that you will never treat your "lover" as you do your present family. Eventually, however, you are apt to behave toward your partner in the way you have learned to deal with your parents, brothers, and sisters. Thus if you desire a loving relationship with a life partner, you should now be seeking improved ways of expressing love toward your family and others around you.

Can anyone be fully successful? Probably not. We all have hate and love feelings which war within us.

But an earnest person can draw upon one more invaluable resource, namely, faith in Christ. In the face of Christ we see the glory of love that paid a supreme price for the well-being of others. In his example we see self-giving at its finest. When we fall short we trust his forgiveness. When we take risks in our effort to love we depend upon his favor.

Those who aspire to be able to love will find that their ability grows through mistakes admitted and corrected. It also grows through practice. Any young person who yearns for the highest joy will studiously seek loving relationships in the inner circle of daily associations. One of the best places to demonstrate our ability to love is our life together in a family.

THE BENEFITS OF LOVE

The story of the first human family is a tragic one, but a revised (and completely unauthorized) script of the happenings in the Garden of Eden may demonstrate the practical benefits of love between a man and woman:

The serpent assured Eve, "When you eat of it your eyes will be opened and you will be like God, knowing good and evil."

Eve considered the serpent's words and replied, "Thank you for telling me. I'll talk with my husband about it and we'll decide what we want to do."

The serpent nodded wisely and lay coiled near the foot of the tree while Eve went to find Adam. She came upon him with his hands full of a new fruit. She told him what she had heard: ". . . and the serpent said that eating the forbidden fruit would make us like God!"

Adam broke off one of the pieces of yellow fruit, opened its peeling, and held it up for Eve to taste. "This tastes good and no one told us we couldn't eat it. Let's wait a while before we violate the orders of the one who put us in this wonderful Garden!"

Eve ate the offered fruit and asked for more. Adam, handing her another piece, continued, "Since you joined me here, this Garden is really paradise! If we honor the Maker and love one another, our life here should be like a dream."

Adam and Eve grew to have deep affection for one another. They were blessed with two sons. One grew up to be a herdsman and the other a farmer. The two young men often talked about their different problems and helped one another in emergencies. They learned to trade fresh meat for newly threshed grain and to share what they produced with their parents.

When the family gathered for a meal one day, Adam offered prayer, thanking the Maker of the Garden for each member of the family and for the abundance which they enjoyed.

"Why so much thankfulness today, Dad?" asked Cain.

"I had a bad dream as I awakened this morning. I dreamed that years ago Eve and I ate the forbidden fruit and had to leave the Garden. The misery of life was almost unbearable. Then the dream shifted and you boys were quarreling and I saw you, Cain, about to strike Abel on the head with a club. I tried to stop you but you hit him. Abel fell to the ground and I knew he was dead. I awakened shuddering . . . uh!"

Eve commented, "I heard you say fiercely, 'No, Cain! No!' I tried to awaken you. Whatever caused you to dream those horrible things?"

"I don't know Dear, but I dread to imagine what our lives might be had they turned out like my dream!"

"I can't think what would make me hit Abel," said Cain. "He and I need each other."

"Perhaps if we had eaten that fruit our lives might have turned out like my dream. I don't know. Knowing good and evil could hardly bless us as much as we have been blessed by learning how to love one another."

How to Reach the Altar

Rachel, age eighteen, leaned against the top of the teacher's desk telling a class of high school girls about herself: "When I was sixteen, a fellow named **Vic** asked me for a date. He drove a sporty car and seemed to have plenty of money. I asked my parents and they warned me not to go. They pointed out that Vic was twenty-one and had a questionable reputation.

"I thought about what they said, but I wanted to go. I had not dated much and the idea of riding in his car and being seen with him just seemed too good to miss.

"We had splendid dates—dinner out, a movie—and then some necking in a quiet place. He quickly moved to heavy petting and clearly wanted more.

"I felt awful, but I didn't have sense enough to bail out. I liked to be wanted. I was on cloud nine with a chance to date. If I refused him, would I lose it all? One night we went all the way and I soon found myself pregnant.

"Now what? I was scared. He agreed to marry me, but we were in deep trouble from the beginning—he had more debts than money. We found a cheap place to rent and drove to another state and got married. The whole thing seemed like a nightmare. Three months after our first date, Vic and I were husband and wife expecting a child.

"We quarreled a lot! I had to quit school. I said many times to myself, 'If this is what marriage is, it's a bummer!'

"The baby came. Soon I was pregnant again. Both my pregnancies were terrible experiences. Vic was gone most of the time. When the second baby came we had three babies in the house—*I was the biggest baby of all!* Vic left me, and my folks let me move back with them.

"Two and a half years ago, I hadn't the wildest dream that my life would go like this. I'm trying to start over again at age eighteen with two small babies. I've enrolled for evening classes to earn the equivalent of a high school diploma. I hope all of you find a better way to go than I did."

Rachel reached the altar unexpectedly at age sixteen. When a young man with an automobile asked her for a date, she was too eager to refuse. Many young people, like Rachel, feel a great urgency to date, to find a partner, and to marry. In the process, careful selectivity in friendships seems like the caution of old folks. One school of thought maintains, "In order to find the handsome prince, you have to kiss a lot of toads."

Such a motto suggests that anyone who is looking for a desirable mate should be ready to date almost anyone who comes along. Supposedly it is better to be dating an unpromising person than not to be dating at all. Rachel's misery after a few delightful dates suggests that the way to the altar is dangerous. Any young person who wants to arrive with high hopes and great joy needs to consider carefully where to start and how to proceed.

THE STARTING PLACE

The best starting place may be labelled "Confident Singlehood." You need to be finding satisfaction in your own life setting as an individual. You need to be at peace with yourself and to be busy about useful and rewarding work and play. Your position for wise choices on your way toward the altar will be stronger if at all times you are content to remain single, even indefinitely or permanently. Many individuals, both men and women, find rich and fulfilling lives without marriage. Traditional religious orders abound with exemplary lives of love and service. Many careers lie open to persons who can devote themselves fully to their work, unrestricted by the responsibilities of a family.

A person in the secure position of confident singlehood can face questions with an open mind:

Do I want to marry?

Am I unsure?

Shall I invite this girl to have a date or shall I wait until I know more about her?

Shall I accept a date with this boy whom I do not know?

Is the person I am dating a prospective mate, or should I look for another?

Freedom to be selective is one of the great advantages of confident singlehood. The rapid and overwhelming drive of passion can be kept at controllable levels if a person is free of the anxiety to be married. The individual thus gains time to complete necessary education, to gain economic independence, and to grow to a desirable level of maturity before trying to make the venture into matrimony.

THE ROUTE OF TRAVEL

From the vantage point of security in single existence, a person can look carefully at the conventional route of travel toward wedded life. There are several stages along the way.

The initial phase is that of dating, a casual relationship in which a man and a woman agree to be together for a few hours on a certain date. Neither person on a single date has an obligation beyond the one occasion agreed upon. The object of being together is to become acquainted and to share a pleasant activity. Many singles try to keep friendships at this level on a very casual basis. Ideally a dating couple builds mutual knowledge of what each one thinks and enjoys.

As acquaintance grows dates may become regular and a

couple is said to be going steady. Again the basic aim in this stage is to discover areas of shared thought and feeling. Through conversation and fun couples discover a rising level of trust. Most couples at this stage of friendship find pleasure in being close together; they experience growing delight in gestures of affection such as hugging and kissing.

Steady dating may eventually merge into courtship, a serious, steady association with definite consideration of life partnership. In this stage each person begins to measure the other as a prospective mate. Visits are planned to introduce each one to the home of the other. Do family members give hearty approval? Does he like her parents and she like his parents? As on the levels of friendship previously mentioned, here too it is desirable to move without haste. A good motto is, "What's the hurry?" A lifetime may last for many years. Extra months devoted to deepening understanding between partners foster trust and increasing joy.

The fourth stage of friendship on the way to the altar is engagement. The couple have promised to marry, and they are publicly recognized as altar-bound. This time is a trial venture for partners-to-be. They appear together at family occasions and test the feelings of others toward their recognized partnership. They lay plans for a wedding and for a home together. Prospects for marital happiness increase with couples whose engagement lasts for several months, a year, or longer.

Without the involvement of full sexual intimacy, the engaged couple finds growing familiarity with one another. They spend enough time together to know their inner feelings, moods, and ways of thinking. Decisions about time and money become a joint activity as they plan for complete merger of resources in marriage.

There is one primary objective of an engagement, namely,

to give a final and thorough test of the suitability of a couple for marriage. This means there is still time to separate if clear evidence indicates that the marriage will be unworkable. Every individual should be alert to avoid mismating. Anyone who sees that a life-union will not be possible should break off a friendship even if wedding plans are already underway. In short, reaching the altar is not the ultimate goal. The goal is rather to reach the altar with confidence in a happy marriage. The engagement is the final testing stage, a time to head off a union which appears to be on a sure collision course.

In his remarkable book *Song of America* George Mardikian tells the story of his experience as a young immigrant from Asia Minor. He recalls his first romance with an American girl. The two of them enjoyed being together. She admired his hard work, his appearance, and his ideas. She found him fun to be with, and he found her very enchanting. As his intensity of feeling for her mounted, it seemed logical to him that he should ask her to marry him. Such a marriage, he reasoned, would be one more step in his becoming a part of his new country.

At this point his brother and his friends began trying to persuade him not to marry the American girl. They pointed out that since she did not know the Armenian language she would always be somewhat of an outsider in his family. She could never share the pleasures of the ethnic group get-togethers. He could never expect her to treat him as a wife treats a husband in the Old World culture. In order to be happy with her he would need to enter her world, learn to be completely at home in it, and leave his own world behind.

Mardikian reports his painful struggle to evaluate himself. Gradually he awakened to the fact that he must break off this friendship. He must wait for a girl who could com-

74 LOVE AND LIVING TOGETHER

prehend his own language, his own culture, and be a part of his Old World and of the new America with him. Through the years that followed that painful separation Mardikian remembered with fondness his first love in America. Eventually he found and grew to love an Armenian girl. They were married and she proved to be a strong and valuable partner, assisting him to become a noted chef and connoisseur of exotic foods.

Some lovers lack the courage to break an engagement and later regret their lack of resolve.

On the night before her wedding **Helen** told a trusted friend that she was deeply afraid. **Glenn** had been quarrelling openly with her father. He seemed to expect her to take his side against her dad. She had seen their mutual distrust earlier, but had hoped things would get better. Glenn had made it clear when he brought her home following the rehearsal dinner that after the wedding she would have to side with him against her father. She had wanted to protest his ultimatum but knew she could not change his mind. They would only have an angry quarrel. She remembered many times when she had kept quiet rather than oppose his rigid ideas. Now she sat in the midst of wedding paraphernalia, her lovely wedding gown, the going away clothes and her partially packed suitcase. She felt utterly trapped—too late to call it off she thought, even though the way ahead was marked by a sign in large letters: DYNAMITE!

PERILS

The route to married life is a treacherous way and individuals who set out on such a journey should be alert for at least three perils:

Antiquated courting roles. By long-standing tradition it is the man in the dating process who has the initiative. He is the one who is supposed to ask for a date. He provides the transportation and pays the bills. If the friendship grows toward marriage, he must take the initiative by proposing marriage. This role placed upon the man has particular dangers. He must risk rejection in order to become acquainted. He must ask for a date and stand exposed while she accepts or refuses. Some men are painfully shy and drift through life without ever taking the initiative required in order to find a life partner.

The girl on her part is spared such a test of courage, but lacking initiative, she must sit back and wait for invitations from men. How does she find male friends in a social situation where initiative is denied? She has to be friendly, attractive, and independent. She has to demonstrate her capacity to live happily alone. She cannot escape from the hazard of her status by asking for a date. If a girl manifests a strong interest in a man, he may back off and avoid her. If she quickly gives her devotion and loyalty to him, he may find all that he wants in her friendship and have no interest in making a proposal of marriage.

It is abundantly clear that we are still functioning with a system based upon the economic and social realities of a century ago. Dating roles that stress male initiative assume that the man is employed, that he has resources to provide transportation and entertainment. The woman, presumably, has no financial resources and can only accept or reject his offer of a date. The first hazard, then, is an antiquated system of romantic courtship that still has binding effects on the way in which young people relate to one another.

Hidden persons. There is a second peril, the peril of the hidden person. Consider the case of a young woman who worked in a city about a hundred miles from her parents:

Sally was excited when **Jake,** whom she met at work, invited her on a date. Sally soon found that she was enjoying dates every night. Jake took her to fine restaurants, to movies, and dances. Her days and nights were a whirl of delight. She enjoyed necking but she refused to go to bed with him. He continually insisted that he loved her and repeatedly asked her to marry him. She put him off saying that they had not known each other long enough. He kept insisting on his desire to marry her, and finally she consented. After a courtship of twelve weeks they were married.

For the first week he was her constant companion. Then his friends began to call or come by. They invited him to go with them to the bar, to play cards, or to attend sporting events. After one month she realized that the every-night companionship she had known while dating had ended. Now she sat alone in their apartment night after night entertaining herself. Jake was always too busy to go with her to visit her parents. The only way she could see her family was to go alone.

Gradually Sally realized that she had married a person who not only cared little for her except for the marriage bed, but also preferred to spend his time in every other way except with her and her family. During courtship Jake had been a counterfeit. He had dressed well. He had left his usual crowd of friends and had given himself totally to her. His actions after marriage led her to conclude that she had been deceived. Sally and Jake separated and obtained a divorce.

How can you avoid the peril of the hidden person who is seeking your friendship? How does a youth see through such pretense and unmask the hidden person? How can you know the real person you'll live with if you marry?

The furniture trap. Consider another peril on the way, that of the furniture trap. Many young people are inclined to get the order of their furniture mixed up. The accepted traditional order is sofa, altar, and bed. When the order is changed to place the bed before the altar, a ceremony at the altar is likely never to occur. Consider the case of a seventeen-year-old girl:

Jackie was not getting along well with her own parents and was attracted to a crowd of young people who had formed a commune some distance from the city where she lived. She went to the commune, but soon found that she wasn't happy with their way of life. She did enjoy the friendship of **Dave,** a boy she met at the commune. They agreed that the place was filthy, so she and Dave rented an apartment and began living together. Jackie suggested that they should get married, but Dave preferred waiting a while. Jackie was in a poor position to bargain so she acceded to his wishes.

Because they did not have enough income from Dave's job, Jackie agreed with their landlord to remove the old paint from the woodwork in their apartment in lieu of one month's rent. The landlord seemed to be pleased with her work. Then one day while she was away from the apartment he painted all the woodwork that she had laboriously stripped. When the apartment was completely redecorated, largely by Jackie's labor, the landlord asked them to leave.

Dave and Jackie found another apartment, also in terrible condition. Jackie struggled to make a home in this new setting. Dave took little interest in her decorating efforts. He liked her cooking but rarely earned enough to buy the food. One day she overheard Dave talking with a friend who asked if Dave hoped to marry Jackie. Dave laughingly replied, "Why buy a cow when you have plenty of milk?"

Jackie was shocked. He was willing to enjoy the benefits of her presence, her help in preparing meals and in keeping a place for him to live, but he didn't care to be a husband. She felt an awful surge of anger rise within her.

Jackie had come to realize that she couldn't get to the altar because she had gotten into bed too soon. She had fallen into the furniture trap. There was nothing to do now but withdraw and hope to begin again, maybe faring better in some new friendship.

SAFE ARRIVAL

The perils we have discussed may be averted if a single person knows how to recognize them. The difficulties of antiquated dating roles may be avoided in newer patterns of group activities. Sororities and fraternities at some universities and colleges schedule group dates—a party that brings together a sorority pledge class and a fraternity pledge class. Individuals can mingle freely, dance with numerous partners, and have conversations with many individuals of both sexes.

Women can offset their lack of formal initiative by participation in church groups, drama projects, sports leagues, and many other activities where friendships may be found. Often older friends arrange introductions for singles enabling them to discover if they would like to become better acquainted. Double dating or group blind dating are alternative arrangements which enable a woman to find new acquaintances.

Most couples drop the old customs once they begin to feel a strong bond of trust. Both can share the cost of a date equally when both are employed. Either may provide transportation when both have automobiles.

The best protection against the counterfeit suitor is ample time for friendship. In early, formal dating a person may hide his or her true habits, but a growing familiarity leaves pretense behind. There are undoubtedly exceptions to the rule, but a friendship span of two years or more spent in dating—going steady—courtship—engagement will allow any couple to know the real person as over against the hidden person seen only romantically on early dates.

The purpose of the studiously protracted system is to provide enough association between a young man and a young woman for them to discover if they are truly compatible. Each individual needs to be alert to assess the suitability of friends of the opposite sex. The following questions may be useful in appraising the person you date:

1. Is he or she genuinely interested in what I think and do?
2. What has this person accomplished?
3. Does my date like me as I am, or try to shape me into another pattern?
4. Is our religious experience and outlook similar?
5. Do we enjoy the same activities?
6. Do we understand and respect each other?
7. Are our life hopes similar?
8. Do we allow each other freedom to speak honestly about any subject?

An unmarried person free of undue urgency to date or to marry has the best chances of making the journey successfully to the altar. He or she can allow ample time, avert the perils along the way, and await a friendship that holds promise for future happiness.

Are You Ready?

Before an airplane pilot takes off he goes through an elaborate procedure. He checks the weather forecasts, studies a map, and works out a flight plan. He files the flight plan with the control tower at the airport. He climbs into his airplane, buckles himself into position, and works the controls of the rudder and wing flaps. He confirms the measure of his fuel supply and tests his navigating instruments. He starts the engine and watches gauges measuring oil pressure and revolutions of the engine per minute. Having used the engine on a primary electrical system, he switches to a reserve electrical system to be sure of its readiness if the first one fails to operate. He moves his plane to an apron near the runway and runs his engines up to full power. He calls the control tower by radio and makes sure that the runway is clear of other aircraft. He double checks the approval of the controller by looking carefully over the flight path. Then, and only then, does he enter the runway and take off.

Air safety results from elaborate preparation by pilots, mechanics, and traffic controllers. Flying is a complex venture which challenges people to prepare carefully and to fly skillfully. Only a fool attempts to fly an airplane without thorough preparation.

For some reason, however, many people suppose that a couple who are in love need no further preparation. In reality, married life is a complex undertaking involving

knowledge and skills which can be learned. Any couple in love need to assess carefully their readiness for marriage. This involves a cooperative search for the answer to two questions:
1. What is marriage?
2. Are we ready to be married?

WHAT IS MARRIAGE?

An ancient definition of Christian marriage states: "A man shall ... be joined to his wife and they shall become one flesh."

The English word *flesh* makes the statement seem an impossibility. Two separate physical bodies cannot be merged into one. The real meaning of the definition is more accurately phrased: "they shall become one."

Marriage is intended to join two individuals into oneness of heart, mind, and body. Considering the character of a human being—a creature distinct from all others, with body, mind, and emotions of its own—marriage looks like a mission impossible. Many male and female pairs fail to move beyond their separate selves into an enduring unity.

How can separate hearts, minds, and bodies be joined together in oneness? Does passionate feeling for one another suffice? No. Can two become one simply by living together? Usually not. Will two individuals achieve oneness by promising to love and honor each other "as long as both shall live"? Even this gives no certainty of a lasting union.

Two human lives become one as they grow together in heart and mind. The gradual process of linking two persons is similar to an early method of constructing a suspension bridge. A kite flown across the chasm and grounded on the other side provided a minimum connection from one side to the other. The kite string was used to pull a fine wire across.

The small wire was used to bring across a larger wire. Eventually, the connecting link was strong enough to pull a heavy cable. Heavy cables hanging from towers on both sides supported the final structure on which traffic moved. Thus, a flimsy kite-string connection ultimately led to a strong bridge.

The ties between a man and woman grow stronger as one strand of trust bears the weight of even stronger strands of confidence and loyalty. This basic trust building accomplishes a joining of lives into a functioning unit. It cannot be hurried or forced. Individual conditioning toward independence must be replaced voluntarily with a desire to depend upon another person. Mechanisms of self-defense widen into defense for two. Restraints on exposure of our bodies to members of the opposite sex cannot be scorned. From earliest childhood we learned to keep ourselves clothed in the presence of other people. Only a mounting level of confidence in another person will allow complete freedom to be seen and touched. In this particular change from aloneness to oneness the wedding ceremony has important psychological benefit.

Over a period of extended friendship with ample time for conversation two separate persons gain the confidence to surrender separateness and bind themselves to one another. As unity grows it releases an inner desire to belong to another person, to possess and be possessed. Mutual commitment between partners often leads to the feeling of ownership beautifully conveyed in a song from the movie, *Friendly Persuasion:* "Thee is mine. Thee pleases me in a hundred ways."

As love grows to this deeper level, it usually yields an ever stronger commitment. Going steady involves an informal bond. The engagement and the wedding involve public acknowledgment of a formal, lasting commitment on the part of two persons to live as one.

Those who venture into complete sexual intimacy before a deep level of trust and commitment is formed may destroy the possibility of genuine unity. Deep guilt feelings may be aroused. Trust is undermined. For most couples early intercourse is awkward if not uncomfortable. For some it proves to be painful. A happy sexual adjustment requires patient learning under optimum conditions of freedom from anxiety. Many young people need the security and social approval which marriage provides to facilitate their progress toward mutual joy in sex.

Doris Day, popular star of movie and television romances, has suggested that living together before marriage is a good way for couples to avoid unhappy marriages. Her own experience, as recounted in *Doris Day: Her Own Story* by A. E. Hotchner, reveals three tragic marriages. She has poignant reason to search for alternatives to the misery she endured. However, her narrative discloses how many of the usual warnings she disregarded. She reportedly married very young twice, married men she did not really know well three times, and never tested any of the liaisons with an adequate engagement period. It seems ironic that she, after her own report of repeated failure, presumes to advise others to disregard society's traditional pattern of preparation for marriage. Her personal description also discloses her disinterest in whether her live-in partner is married or single. Thus she apparently endorses both unchastity and adultery.

Youth who are seeking happiness in an enduring marital union need to be very careful in assessing the advice and example of individuals whose marital experience has been unhappy. A wiser course would include careful observation of the lives of a happily married man and woman. Perhaps a couple preparing for marriage could interview a happy husband and wife to learn how they achieved and maintained oneness.

A vast body of knowledge is also available from scientific research about marriage. Statistically, couples are likely to form stronger marriages if they:

1. Have similar ethnic and religious upbringing.
2. Are twenty-two years of age or older.
3. Have both had college education.
4. Have a sound economic base in the earning skills of one or both partners.
5. Have dated widely before becoming engaged.
6. Have gone steady over an extended period of time.
7. Have been engaged from one to two and one-half years.
8. Share hopes for a home and children.

Some readers may object that many couples are happily married who did not meet one or more of these standards. The objection has some validity, but enduring marital happiness is still more probable for a pair who fit the criteria. Careful selectivity, maturity, ample years of association, and a sound income base have more bearing upon long-run satisfaction in living together than does the intensity of any romantic feelings.

Audrey told her father when he came to the campus that she had found a completely new chapter in her life since she had been dating **Fred:** "Fred and I are growing together steadily, Dad. We are not hurrying into anything. We talk a lot and find that we agree on so many things that it seems uncanny. We study together and have fun together. We are finding more and more confidence in our future. What we are building is too precious to take chances."

Audrey and Fred had come to a realistic understanding of marriage. They were patiently and joyfully building unity of heart and mind.

PREPARING FOR MARRIAGE

A couple in love should be certain they are ready to be married. Marriage counselors and social scientists have added richly to our understanding of marital happiness and have provided useful equipment to aid a couple in preparing for wedded life. Tools for testing the suitability of a couple for marriage are widely available. If you and your loved one truly wish to assess your readiness, you should focus on four questions:

How can we test our knowledge of one another? James R. Hine, a veteran marriage counselor, has produced a useful manual entitled *Grounds for Marriage* which provides a system for a couple to test their acquaintance with each other. It assists them in reviewing their motives for wanting to marry. It includes checklists on viewing and listening pleasure, sports, hobbies, and attitudes towards life. It offers charts for comparison of personality profiles. Even couples who use the manual after lengthy courtship frequently discover new information about one another.

Do we share ideas about marriage and family life? Dr. Hine has provided a companion tool in the form of a card game built around eighty-five provocative statements about marriage and family life. The game is played by a couple sitting opposite each other. Each individual reacts independently to each statement. Then they compare their answers and discuss the differences and similarities of their opinions. Finally they compare their ideas with those of a marriage counselor whose printed answers cite sociological data regarding marriage. The score sheet can be compared with standardized results based upon the number of agreements and disagreements of one thousand couples whose scores have been averaged.

Couples using this tool testify that it is fun and that it gives them confidence to learn that they share a large measure of agreement about marriage. Areas of disagreement are identified for further study and discussion.

How do we feel about our togetherness? You may evaluate the way you experience life together by asking a series of questions:

Is your relationship an easy one? When you are with the other person do you feel free? Are you free to share your hurts, your weaknesses, and your attainments? Can you be yourself?

Is your relationship an honest one? Do you have to pretend? Do you have to play roles when you are with each other? Is it fair? Does one person have to do all the running and chore work, while the other one sits around and accepts the benefits of another's service?

Is it deep? Does it seem to have deep, flowing, inner strength? Do you sense a quiet trust between you, a sacred inner reality that is not built but discovered? Do you sense harmony so pervasive that your two personalities seem to be one? Does this oneness find expression in shared devotion? In prayer? In the pleasure of worship together? Shared religious experience often verifies and enhances the trust that has developed between two people.

Is it fun? Is your work more joyous when shared? Is silence pleasant? Do you play? Can you pick a buttercup together or walk in the rain? Can you experiment with a special casserole for a meal together? Do you enjoy a picnic?

Does pleasure require the spending of money and elaborate amusement or is there joy in simple everyday activity? Is it refreshing to be near one another?

Do we know how to use power? The most crucial factor in measuring readiness for marriage is a couple's shared knowledge about the use of power. Marriage tradition of many centuries assigned authority in the marriage to the man. This assignment became part of the marriage contract with separately worded vows. The husband promised to love and *honor* the wife. The wife promised to love and *obey* her husband. Such vows were undoubtedly used by some men to justify male tyranny in the family.

However, those who lament the injustices of traditional marriage need to note that tyranny and love are incompatible. A tyrant may force a subject to yield physical obedience but he cannot by so doing win and enjoy love. A strong woman may compel a husband to fulfill her outward command but she cannot make him regard her tenderly. Whatever outward appearance may have suggested about male-dominated families, the highest joys of mutual love could only be known where lovers were considered partners. Genuine sharing of affection is a two-way activity that is founded upon mutual confidence in the joint use of power. In modern marriage few couples try to maintain the dominant-male image. Marriage partners expect to share power. Each assumes that his or her opinions will be weighed carefully in making joint decisions. Confidence in the shared use of power is an essential ingredient in effective teamwork between spouses.

When two people measure their readiness for marriage and discover the shared use of power, happiness in being together, a common understanding of marriage, and a thorough knowledge of one another, they may move toward wedded life with assurance that they have a high marriage-happiness quotient. Their careful preparation for uniting their lives yields a good prospect for enduring love.

Can Love Survive?

One popular attitude toward marriage in the twentieth century has been voiced in the words of a song:

> I've got spurs that jingle, jangle, jingle
> As I go riding merrily along,
> And they say, "Oh, ain't you glad you're single?"
> And that song ain't so very far from wrong!

Newspaper headlines often indicate an increasing tendency for people to escape from, or to avoid matrimony:

> "Marriage Institution Fares Poorly in Census Study"
> "One-Person Households Jump 29%"
> "Million Unmarried Couples Living Together"
> "Millions of Unmarried Americans Creating New Lifestyle"

Each of these headlines introduced data suggesting that marriage is in trouble.

IS MARRIAGE ON THE WAY OUT?

There is abundant evidence that marriage is here to stay. The American Institute of Insurers recently released the findings of a poll of the life aims of adults. The survey revealed that 90% of all Americans consider marriage and family as their primary life goal. Unmarriage is not displacing marriage. Approximately 2.3 million couples march up the aisle to form covenants of marriage annually. In a recent six-year period the average annual increase in marriages among Americans was fifty-four thousand, almost matching the increase in unmarriages in the same years.

Despite many evidences of discontent with marriage, Americans displayed little confidence in living together unmarried. It has been indicated that the number of couples living together unmarried increased to 957,000—almost double the number reported a few years earlier. However, even with this rapid increase, the unmarried cohabitants were still an infinitesimally small percentage of all the men and women living together.

The upsurge of unmarriage in America appears to have been a temporary outgrowth of the rebellious mood of students in the years of the Vietnam War. In the mid-seventies the number of youthful unmarried cohabitants apparently began to decline. Stories of the unhappiness of unmarried couples living together began spreading among younger acquaintances. At one large university cohabitation by unmarried students rose to a high of 22% and then dropped to 16% in the late seventies.

National media coverage of alternate living arrangements may lead to the impression that marriage will cease to be as important for couples in love as it has been in earlier times. The doubling of the divorce rate in a twelve-year interval appeared to depict the same dismal outlook for marriage. That impression, however, is not supported by the facts. Marital disappointment and divorce have very little impact upon the intention of individuals to marry. William M. Ramsey, writing in the independent religious publication *Presbyterian Outlook,* stated: "A divorced person is more likely to marry [again] than a person of the same age who has never been married. In spite of our many divorces there are thirty married people for every divorced adult who has still not remarried. People want to be married."

Anyone evaluating marriage needs to bear in mind that the majority of marriages endure. Two of every three couples succeed in wedded life. In certain portions of society marriage success runs much higher. Surveys reveal that the marriage stability of families who go regularly to church stands above 95%. Society has become more tolerant of unmarried individuals who live together, but its overall affirmation of marriage is clear. Love is flourishing in enough marriages to influence an overwhelming proportion of people to prefer marriage above any other lifestyle.

Within a recent five-year period the number of one-person households increased 29%. Does this indicate people's growing preference to live alone? Not necessarily. Those who live alone fall primarily into two groups—those who have lost their spouses, and the unmarried. The census reports indicate that an increasing number of young adults establish separate households, and that many young people are delaying marriage until an older age.

Affluence may be one of the contributing factors in the increase of separate households for young singles; that is, their ability to finance separate living quarters may be more important in their behavior than opposition to marriage. In any case the trend may prove to be beneficial for their eventual happiness in marriage. Independence and maturity enable people to be more selective in their choice of mates and to be better qualified for success in marriage. The trend toward living alone is a sign of change in the society, but it may very well foreshadow an era of greater stability for married couples. In the short run more people are living alone, but this does not gainsay their preference to marry when they find a promising opportunity.

Thus the prospects for marriage are bright. Changes in living arrangements are taking place, but the vast majority of people prefer marriage.

ADVANTAGES OF MARRIAGE

Why do people prefer marriage? Most people prefer marriage because it has certain inherent advantages. It offers a cluster of benefits that no other living arrangement can provide. It combines love and companionship with security and family. These inherent advantages of marriage deserve a careful review.

Marriage provides internal cohesion and external support which are not available to the unmarried. In the wedding the bride and groom formally affirm the loyalty they feel toward one another. Each one says in effect, "I'm not going to leave you. You can count on me when we are happy *and* when we are in trouble." In most marriages this commitment joins two lives as one. Confidence and feelings of security in such a union are an indispensable asset. The couple, while retaining their individuality, function as one. Their internal cohesion is renewed daily through affection. It is fortified by full and honest conversation. It proves itself in harmonious sharing of authority. It remains steadfast when disputes—even heated arguments—arise. When the going is rough, such a couple know that the fundamental oneness of their life together remains unbroken. The trust level of oneness between two partners sustains a married couple when two other persons who live together without a lasting commitment split and go their separate ways.

The married couple also benefits by external support that

is unique. A Christian wedding ceremony can be a key element in such support. The bride and groom make their vows in the presence of God and the assembled company. The ceremony publicly displays the formation of a *three-way* covenant between the two persons being wed and God. Their promises to one another are also promises to God who is asked to bless and sustain their union. One wedding prayer includes a petition for "the seal" of God's approval and his "fatherly benediction."

This religiously-based covenant is supported through the devotional life of the couple and by their fellowship in a congregation. Couples who pray together frequently find that their covenant with God in marriage is a rich source of inspiration and strength. Mutual forgiveness and renewal in times of stress further reward those who trust in their sacred unity with God.

No one should underestimate the value of a supporting community or congregation. In the house of worship and in the homes of the family and other members of the congregation the couple is welcomed with hearty approval. Two people may suppose that their living arrangements are not subject to any one else's opinion, but most of us, even after we leave our parents' homes, return to childhood homes for the festive occasions of the year—Christmas, Easter, and Thanksgiving as well as family celebrations of anniversaries and birthdays. A cordial, approving welcome to both partners is a delightful boon. The new family member by marriage has a place of honor and respect. Through internal cohesion and external support, a married couple have valuable resources for the survival of love between them.

Another major benefit flows to spouses from the superb opportunity which they enjoy to give health and increased effectiveness to one another. Douglas H. Heath, a professor of psychology at Haverford College, has released his findings from an intensive, thirteen-year study of sixty professional men. He found that maritally happy individuals are more mature and more effective professionally than other men. When the men being studied were asked to explain their health and professional effectiveness they unanimously gave credit to their wives. Consider the responses of two men:

1. "I relate better to other people in my daily work because I relate better to my wife."

2. "She's helped me to learn what I don't have to be. I don't have to be deadly serious about everything that I do. She has helped me to have fun, to laugh at myself. She's challenged me when I've been pompous or pedantic or petty. She's really made me feel that no matter what happens she will stand with me and by me, and that gives me a great sense of security and confidence in what I do."

Precisely comparable research on how men affect the well-being of women is not available, but it may be assumed that a similar study of women's health and well-being would yield comparable findings. When two people unite their lives in a lasting commitment, they can provide benefits to one another that far outweigh day-to-day living arrangement.

Marriage also has an inherent advantage in assuring the health and happiness of children. A loving couple bound to one another in a covenant of marriage are uniquely qualified to become partners in creation. Through an act of love between them they initiate a new life which they cherish from the moment of conception. Later they joyously welcome their son or daughter at birth and surround him or her with love, legal identity, and family security.

CAN LOVE SURVIVE? 95

John and **Sue,** the couple who decided against living together unwed, were married a year later. After their honeymoon they moved to a city where John located a better job. Two years later Sue wrote to her pastor:

Dear Mr. Smith,

I have been wanting to write you for several months. John and I appreciate what you have done for us. Our wedding was lovely and your kindness stands as an especially pleasant memory.

What we really want you to know is that we owe you a debt we can never repay. When you came to the apartment two years ago you found us preparing to live together. We resented your coming that night but you did not scold or blame us. You let us explain what we were doing and, as we talked, I began to see how foolish it was. Then you talked about the promises of marriage.

As you know, we later made those promises, and we're very happy! I hate to think about what would have occurred if you had not come that night. The love we now share might have failed. After you left we decided to wait and we know that our love has grown stronger.

Yesterday John and I learned that we are going to have a baby! Our lives will be joined in a new life and our promises to each other will then assure love and care for our child.

We thank God every day for our lives together and we thank you for being around when we needed you most.

With loving appreciation,
Sue and John

Beside the inherent advantages of marriage—partnership in creation, the health-giving power of spouses, and the cohesion and support which marriage provides for love—modern marriage offers special advantages:

1. The arranged marriage of older times has given way to marriage based on friendship and love between two people.
2. The man-dominant home has largely vanished in favor of partnerships between equals.

3. Much ignorance and superstition about sex has been dispelled.
4. The drudgery of housekeeping has been greatly reduced.
5. Women enjoy a wide range of opportunity for education and employment, making marriage an option rather than a necessity.
6. Marriages where love breaks down can usually be dissolved through divorce.
7. Child care centers give little children educational advantages while offering parents the option for both to be employed outside the home.
8. Old traditions of breadwinner-man and housekeeper-woman have yielded to a flexible division of duties in child care, other domestic tasks, and income-yielding employment.
9. Safe and effective birth control relieves the former burdens of parents with large families and allows spouses greater opportunity for joy in sexual intimacy.
10. Parenthood is now optional—meaning that people can accept such responsibility as a privilege rather than an almost inevitable consequence of marriage.
11. Dangerous pregnancies can be safely and lawfully terminated.

Thus marriage, which has always offered advantages over any other arrangement for living together, has been improved by the elimination of many causes of unhappiness in the past. The opportunities for happiness in marriage have never been better. Modern marriages have become largely dependent upon love rather than economic or social necessity.

Why then are so many people experiencing disappointment in marriage? The answer lies in the wonder and mystery of love between the sexes. Most of us instinctively seek to find love in living together with a person of the opposite sex. Security in living together, however, requires the ability to love on an enduring basis. Marriage offers the best arrangement we have for sustaining and renewing love.

And still some succeed while others fail. In *The Sound of Music* there is an unforgettable lyric about hardships in famous love affairs. The lovers lament their lack of problems such as crowded quarters and dearth of money, asking in jest, "How can love survive?"

Although the words, in a humorous way, testify to the durability of love, the closing question, "How can love survive?" is in the minds of many unmarried people. In the latter part of the twentieth century, how can love survive?

YOUR SEARCH FOR ENDURING LOVE

How can your love survive? You can find love that endures if you learn how to give yourself in intelligent and responsible concern for others. This involves an understanding of yourself, of your life hopes, and of your capacity both socially and sexually to give happiness to others. It includes awareness of your own worth and attention to the well-being of others. You can discover, learn, and practice the art of loving.

When you have learned to love, you have good prospects to find a mate with whom you can share even richer joys of loving. You can recognize the advantages of marriage and be prepared to deal with any perils you may encounter en route to the altar.

In your search for enduring love with another person you will wisely:

1. Begin a friendship gently.

2. Focus initially upon fun as companions, with plenty of time for talking to one another.
3. Advance tenderly in affection.
4. Allow ample time in courtship.
5. Test your love ideally through a year or more of engagement.
6. Incorporate your love in a covenant of marriage.
7. Consummate it joyfully in the ecstasy of your honeymoon.
8. Renew it daily in thoughtful words and deeds.
9. Dedicate it to the future by becoming partners in starting new life.

It is difficult to imagine any finer way to fulfill your personhood than through such a venture in living together. May you be able to rejoice daily in the privileges of enduring love.

> Love knows no limit to its endurance, no end to its trust, no fading of its hope. It is, in fact, the one thing that still stands when all else has fallen. . . . Follow, then, the way of love.

Appendixes

THE BIBLICAL TEACHINGS ON SEX

Young people in the twentieth century may wonder if rules about sex that were established thousands of years ago can still form a valid basis for behavior. The biblical rules frequently quoted by adults sound both ancient and repressive: "Thou shalt not commit adultery" (Exod. 20:14); "The unrighteous shall not inherit the kingdom . . . neither fornicators, nor idolaters, nor adulterers . . ." (1 Cor. 6:9).

Thoughtful youth will avoid hasty disdain for teachings, however ancient, that were designed to protect a strong and cohesive system of family life. Anyone in the modern era who wants to make intelligent choices about a sexual lifestyle will want to consider carefully the wisdom of such counsel about marriage and the family.

According to Hebrew tradition God made man and woman, saw that his creation was good, and instructed the first people to "multiply and fill the earth" (Gen. 1:28, 31). The man was directed to leave his parents and be loyal to his wife, the two becoming "one flesh" (Gen. 2:24). A strict code of behavior was developed to safeguard the married couple and to assure the well-being of the family. Hebrew law protected spouses and children against incest, adultery, and rape. Severe penalties were established against promiscuous sexual activity.

In the New Testament, these ancient Hebrew ideals for the family were preserved, but the emphasis went beyond specific laws regulating particular acts. Deeds came to be measured by higher standards:
1. the motives which lay behind them,
2. the fruits which resulted from them, and
3. neighborly love which responsibly sought the well-being of other persons.

All people were invited to enter a new way of love in which each person, instead of exalting self through conquest or exploitation of others, tried to deny or sacrifice self for the sake of others. Each believer was enjoined to subordinate the passions of the flesh in order to attain a higher righteousness founded upon love for God and neighbor. Sexual intercourse was reserved for married couples through whom it could yield blessings to the present generation and to their posterity.

Young people were advised to revere their bodies, viewing them as the temples of God's Spirit (1 Cor. 3:16). This meant to practice chastity before marriage and fidelity to one another in the sexual pleasures of wedded life. Youth were urged: "Let no one despise your youth, but set the believers an example . . . in love, in faith, in purity (1 Tim. 4:12); "shun youthful passions and aim at righteousness, faith, love, and peace" (2 Tim. 2:22).

The biblical teachings about sex are sometimes negatively expressed, and they have often been perpetuated in a legalistic manner. Nonetheless, they intend positive support for a noble ideal of personal behavior and marital happiness. Twentieth-century youth may wisely search out this heritage and lay claim to its benefits.

ALTERNATIVES FOR UNMARRIED COUPLES LIVING TOGETHER

If you are living together unmarried, you have three obvious alternatives:

1. You may continue to cohabit as you are,
2. You may marry, or
3. You may separate.

In examining these alternatives you should ask yourselves at least two questions:

1. Are we happy together?
2. Does our living-together arrangement satisfy our long-range hopes?

You may discover that the two of you cannot give the same answers to these questions. One person may be heartily content to live indefinitely on a day-to-day basis, while the other yearns for a lasting partnership. (Sometimes the woman entertains the hope that she can provide her companion enough pleasure and comfort that he will desire to marry, but the prospects of entering marriage by this course of action are seldom good.) If you cannot readily answer yes to both of these questions, each of you may need to pursue several individual considerations:

Do I want a lasting companionship with a trusted mate?

Do I want to establish a home?

Do I hope to have children?

If either of you desires such benefits of marriage, you need to talk together frankly about your hopes for the future. If both of you agree to be married you may wish to work with a pastor to write a ceremony in which you consecrate the love you already hold for one another.

If your present partnership does not satisfy your life-hopes you should weigh carefully the possibility and the timing of separation. This may be difficult, even painful, but it does open the way for new friendships.

If you separate and return to a single lifestyle, you may wisely consider two standards of conduct in dating:

1. Accept repeated dates only with persons who eventually intend to marry, and
2. Reserve sexual intimacy until after the wedding.

May you find happiness in your search for enduring love and loyalty.

Notes

Page
12 "Two-person households": Figures from the population division of the United States Census Bureau, as reported in the *Philadelphia Evening Bulletin,* 20 October 1977.
14 "Divorce rate": Census Bureau, *Jacksonville Courier,* 25 February 1977.
"Homicide survey": Rollo May, *Power and Innocence* (New York: W.W. Norton and Co., 1972), p. 115.
"Newton-John": *Chicago Tribune Magazine,* 12 September 1976.
15 "The American family": Norman Mailer, "The Search for Carter," *New York Times Magazine,* 26 September 1976, p. 76.
16 "The bounds of matrimony": Lawrence Casler, *Is Marriage Necessary?* (New York: Human Sciences Press, 1974), p. 116
"Marriage . . . has failed": M.L. Cadwallader, in ibid., p. 144.
20 "Singles": *Jacksonville Courier,* 17 March 1976.
23 "Fornication laws": "Living Together," *Newsweek,* 1 August 1977.
24 "Survey on living together": Peter Lindberg, "What's Happening to the American Family?" *Better Homes and Gardens,* October 1972, p. 52.
"Carter": *National Observer,* 30 May 1977.

104 LOVE AND LIVING TOGETHER

25 "Eleven cohabiting couples": A personal interview with Duane Heap, October 12, 1976.

26 "Ann Landers": *Jacksonville Courier,* 17 January 1977.
"Rita": *National Observer,* 18 November 1975.
"Survival record": *Jacksonville Courier,* 21 November 1976; also a personal interview, September 28, 1977.

27 "College cohabitants survey": Joyce Brothers, *Good Housekeeping,* August 1975, p. 49.
"Newlywed and dating couples survey": A personal interview with Alfred Heasty, November 28, 1976.

28 "Soviet marriage patterns": Michel Gordey, *Visa to Moscow* (New York: Alfred A. Knopf, 1952), p. 81.
"Soviet physicians": *St. Louis Post-Dispatch,* 3 October 1976.

29 "Unhappy stories about . . . cohabiting": Louise Montague, *Reader's Digest,* April 1977, p. 94.

37 "Sixty-one teenage boys": Daniel Offer and Judith Backin Offer, "Like Father, Like Son," *Family Health,* August 1976, p. 8.
"'Who's Who' survey": *Jacksonville Courier,* 27 November 1975.

38 "Sexual revolution a myth": As quoted in Henry A. Bowman, *Marriage for Moderns* (New York: McGraw-Hill, 1974), p. 47.

39 "The pill": Ronald L. Kleinman, *Family Planning Handbook for Doctors* (London: International Planned Parenthood Federation, 1974), p. 60.
"VD epidemic": Jules Saltman, "VD-Epidemic among Teenagers," *Public Affairs Pamphlet,* no. 517 (New York: Public Affairs Committee, 1974), p. 17.

55 "Masters and Johnson": William H. Masters and Virginia E. Jonson, *The Pleasure Bond* (Toronto: Bantam Books, 1974), pp. 283-84.

"C. S. Lewis": C. S. Lewis, *Christian Behavior* (New York: Macmillan Co., 1945), p. 30.

61 "Age of Puberty": Fred E. Deatherage, *Food for Life* (New York: Plenum Press, 1975), p. 108.

73 "Mardikian": George Mardikian, *Song of America* (New York: McGraw-Hill, 1956), p. 83.

83 "Doris Day": A.E. Hotchner, *Doris Day: Her Own Story* (New York: Bantam Books, 1975), pp. 56–59, 88–90, 97, 134–40, 270–71, 340–41.

84 "Stronger marriages": Evelyn Willis Duvall and Reuben Hill, *When You Marry* (New York: Association Press, 1948), pp. 101, 118–21, 431–38. See also Ray Baber, *Marriage and the Family* (New York: McGraw-Hill, 1939), pp. 176–81, 195–99.

85 "Grounds for marriage": James R. Hine, *Grounds for Marriage* (Danville, Ill.: Interstate Printers and Publishers, 1971), pp. 3 ff.

89 "Headlines": *Jacksonville Courier*, 7 January 1976; 17 March 1976; 10 February 1977; *U.S. News and World Report*, 31 January 1977.

"Life-aims survey": Institute of Insurers, *Women's Interest*, January-February 1975, p. 3.

90 "Increase in marriages": *Vital Statistics of the United States, 1973* (Rockwell, Md.: Department of Health, Education, and Welfare, 1977), pp. 1–7; and *Statistical Abstract of the United States, 1976*, 97th ed. (Washington: The United States Census Bureau, 1976), p. 68.

"The mid-seventies . . . decline": A personal interview with Nancy Moore Clatworthy, referred to above in note concerning p. 30.

91 "People want to be married": William M. Ramsey, "Men, Women, and God," *Presbyterian Outlook*, 13 June 1977.

"Marriage success": "At Long Last Marriage," *Spectator*, March 1977, p. 4.

"One person households": *Jacksonville Courier*, 17 March 1976.

94 "Sixty professional men": Douglas H. Heath, "Will Marriage Survive?" *Thesis Theological Cassettes* (Pittsburgh: Thesis, 1977), vol. 8, no. 5.

98 "The way of love": 1 Corinthians 13:7, 8; 14:1 (Phillips translation).

Suggestions for Further Reading

There are books which interpret clearly and candidly the meaning and practical reality of sex for youth and young adults. Some of them are mentioned here.

Cole, William Graham. *Sex and Love in the Bible.* New York: Association Press, 1959, 437 pages. Provides a thorough review of biblical teachings about sex and a history of how those teachings have been applied to standards of behavior.

Duvall, Evelyn Millis. *Love and the Facts of Life.* New York: Association Press, 1966, 352 pages. Interprets the meaning of sex in early friendship, dating, courtship, and marriage.

Duvall, Evelyn Millis. *Why Wait Till Marriage?* New York: Association Press, 1970, 128 pages. A down-to-earth analysis of sexual relationships among youth, providing substantial reasons to "wait until marriage."

Duvall, Evelyn M. and Sylvanus M. *Sense and Nonsense about Sex.* New York: Association Press, 1962, 124 pages. Clear and honest answers to questions raised by youth, revealing much of the romantic nonsense about sex which confuses modern youth.

Fromm, Erich. *The Art of Loving.* New York: Bantam Books, 1963, 118 pages. A noted psychoanalyst's "daring prescription for love," with useful guidance about learning how to love.

Hettlinger, Richard F. *Growing Up with Sex.* New York: Seabury Press, 1971, 162 pages. Offers high school youth honest and practical answers to questions about sex during adolescent years.

Hettlinger, Richard F. *Living with Sex: The Student's Dilemma.* New York: Seabury Press, 1966, 185 pages. Candid discussion of various forms of premarital sex, offering valuable guidance to college-age readers.

Hine, James R. *Grounds for Marriage.* Danville, Illinois: The Interstate Printers and Publishers, Inc., 1971, 85 pages. A practical manual to enable a couple who contemplate marriage to evaluate their "grounds" for joining their lives in wedlock, provided by many pastors as a basic tool in premarital counseling with couples.

Kirkendall, Lester A. *Premarital Intercourse and Interpersonal Relationships.* New York: Gramercy Publishing Co., 1961, 302 pages. The experiences of 200 unmarried college males in 668 sexual intercourse situations, evaluated in terms of what consequently happened to the interpersonal relationships of the participants.

Mace, David R. *Youth Considers Marriage.* Camden: Thomas Nelson & Sons, 1969, 94 pages. A veteran marriage counselor's discussion of questions which unmarried young people confront, with recommendations that can lead toward enduring happiness in Christian marriage.

Mace, David and Vera. *We Can Have Better Marriages If We Really Want Them.* Nashville: Abingdon Press, 1974, 172 pages. Evaluates modern marriage alongside alternative lifestyles, heartily affirms monogamy, and describes a growing variety of resources for marriage enrichment.

Ogg, Elizabeth. *Unmarried Teenagers and Their Children.* New York: Public Affairs Pamphlets, 1976, 28 pages. With out-of-wedlock births now approaching one-half million annually, this booklet candidly describes the multiple personal and social consequences of parenthood without marriage.

Stirling, Nora. *You Would If You Loved Me.* New York: Avon Books, 1969, 175 pages. A sensitive novel about teenagers confronting the realities of "going all the way."

Wood, Frederic C., Jr. *Sex and the New Morality.* New York: Association Press, 1968, 157 pages. Analyzes the ethical involvements of modern, young adults and sets forth guidelines for making decisions about sexual behavior.

"Sexuality and the Human Community," Report of a Task Force of the General Assembly of the United Presbyterian Church in the United States of America, Philadelphia, Pa., 1970, 56 pages. Sheds light on "man's perennial confusion about the meaning of sex," and evaluates biblical teachings, traditional sex ethics, and modern reality.

Acknowledgments

I am grateful to Dr. Roland Tapp who initiated me into writing for publication, and to a host of people who contributed ideas and encouragement for the writing of this book. Individuals whose helpfulness should be recognized are: Mary Manlove, Lawrence and Carolyn Crawford, Alfred Henderson, Margaret Fox, Betsy Robb, Bernard Fuhr, Bob Jamison, Viola Winn, Dick and Mary Jean McGuire, and Janet Bair, and also Arlene, Darel, and Ronda Robb. Virginia Green skillfully converted piles of rough copy into neat typescript.

Dale Robb